New Students in Two-Year Colleges

New Students in Two-Year Colleges

Twelve Essays

Edited by

Walker Gibson
University of Massachusetts—Amherst

National Council of Teachers of English
1111 Kenyon Road, Urbana, Illinois 61801

Southern Baptist College
FELIX GOODSON
LIBRARY
Walnut Ridge, Ark.

NCTE Editorial Board: Evelyn Copeland, Rudine Sims, Donald C. Stewart, Ann Terry, Frank Zidonis, Robert F. Hogan, *ex officio*, Paul O'Dea, *ex officio*

Book Design: Tom Kovacs

NCTE Stock Number 33452

Copyright © 1979 by the National Council of Teachers of English. All rights reserved. Printed in the United States of America.

It is the policy of NCTE in its journals and other publications to provide a forum for the open discussion of ideas concerning the content and the teaching of English and language arts. Publicity accorded to any particular point of view does not imply endorsement by the Executive Committee, the Board of Directors, or the membership at large, except in announcements of policy, where such endorsement is clearly specified.

Library of Congress Cataloging in Publication Data

Main entry under title:

New students in two-year colleges.

    Bibliography: p.
    1. English philology—Remedial teaching—
Addresses, essays, lectures. 2. English language
—Rhetoric—Study and teaching—Addresses, essays,
lectures. 3. Community colleges—United States—
Addresses, essays, lectures. I. Gibson, Walker.
PE66.N4   808'.007'1173   78-31164
ISBN 0-8141-3345-2

48594

P
808.007
N42

Contents

Acknowledgments

Grateful acknowledgment is made for permission to reprint the following poems: "Ceremony" and untitled poem from *Ceremony* by Leslie Silko. Copyright © 1977 by Leslie Silko. Reprinted by permission of Viking Penguin Inc. "Sand Creek" by Charles Ballard; "Chrome Babies Eating Chocolate Snowmen in the Moonlight," "Written in Unbridled Repugnance Near Sioux Falls, Alabama—April 30, 1974," and "Sitting Bull's Will Versus the Sioux Treaty of 1868 and Monty Hall" by A. K. Redwing; and "Indian Song: Survival" by Leslie Silko from *Voices of the Rainbow*, edited by Kenneth Rosen. Copyright © 1975 by Kenneth Rosen. Reprinted by permission of Viking Penguin Inc. "Manifest Destiny," "Eclipse," and "Red Rock Ceremonies" by Anita Endrezze Probst from *Carriers of the Dream Wheel*, edited by Duane Niatum. Copyright 1975 by Harper & Row, Publishers, Inc. Reprinted by permission of the author. "D-Y Bar" by James Welch from *Carriers of the Dream Wheel*, edited by Duane Niatum. Copyright 1975 by Harper & Row, Publishers, Inc. Reprinted by permission of the author.

Introduction

During the academic year 1976–77, twelve professors of English from two-year colleges lived and studied at the University of Massachusetts in Amherst. They were engaged in a seminar entitled "Reading and Writing in the First College Years," having been selected for this purpose in a nationwide competition. The seminar was made possible by a grant from the Fellowships Division of the National Endowment for the Humanities.

As director of this seminar, I felt constrained to introduce the Fellows to a modest critical vocabulary with some readings in linguistics and style, and to an approach to writing and teaching familiar to graduates of similar enterprises I have conducted recently. But a funny thing happened. Whether it was because of the relatively long duration of this particular project or because of the energies of this elite group, they began, well before Christmas, to take things into their own capable hands. Each Fellow had arrived bearing plans for independent research, ranging from pedagogical interests to standard literary scholarship. As the autumn wore on, the individuality of these activities faded in the interests of a common concern: the teaching of English in the two-year college. Without abandoning their various scholarly enterprises, the Fellows nevertheless began to see, in constant interchange with one another, that their shared commitment to their professional obligations offered a common subject that deserved to have their united attention, there and then.

During that frigid winter, then, their papers were drafted and redrafted, grouped and regrouped, discussed and edited. The result is this collection, addressed to other college teachers of English, purporting to say what we think we know about the teaching of reading and writing to certain "new" kinds of students now familiar in the two-year college and elsewhere.

The traditionally trained professor in college or university (like me) will find some of these statements surprising, not to say alarming. To responsibly teach the "new student" is not to water down traditional approaches; it is to do something different. Take a single example: the study of literature in this instance is not a display of works of art, structures of language to be noted and admired. As Theresa Enroth and others point out, content is paramount, for their students believe that if you ask them to read an author, then you believe that what that author says about how to live should be taken seriously. Distinguishing between art and life, so crucial to our traditional academic concerns with literature, has to be postponed, or abandoned altogether. These teachers repeatedly ask themselves: What might conceivably be worthwhile in the twenty-first century to the student who will not be a reader of literature? And the opportunity provided by our grant meant that we could face some theoretical implications of that question and its various answers.

We begin, then, with the students. James R. Doherty offers a profile of the new student—in his instance, one who scores in the lowest third on various national tests of ability and aptitude. Rejecting a number of approaches that in effect are devices for keeping such students shackled in lower-class positions, Doherty takes high ground. "Rather than lowering our educational goals, and the students' aspirations, we should rearrange the world to fit the needs of the students." If this seems an unlikely possibility, the impulse nevertheless animates much of the advice that Doherty's colleagues offer to teachers of the new students.

It should be added that the student bodies served by these twelve colleges are anything but monolithic. But some characteristics are possessed more or less in common by those we are here calling new students. They form a familiar list. The new students are poor at taking tests, they lack self-confidence in classroom situations, they expect failure. They are job-oriented to the point of being anti-intellectual. Their own economic survival is much on their minds. They don't read very much. In sum, these are people who, a generation ago, would not have found themselves in institutions called colleges. But the teachers who are writing in these essays, far from deploring or bemoaning the presence of such students, are determined to provide them with an education in English that is supportive and practical—and based on the best possible linguistic and pedagogical principles.

The second paper reminds us of the way in which misused scientific terminology and procedures damage our teaching. James J. Kinney urges English teachers to find their salvation in themselves and not in "scientism."

There follow six fairly practical proposals for attaining such salvation. The first two deal mainly with method. Theresa L. Enroth discusses the various appeals that fiction can provide for the new student. They are far from the traditional lit-crit appeals familiar to academe. In a related paper, Susan R. Blau suggests a personal approach to literature, emphasizing the real-life author and flying in the face of the intentional-biographical "fallacy."

The next four papers address themselves to various kinds of material appropriate for new-student classrooms. Marsha M. Oliver defends the use of popular "formula fiction" for students who are unprepared for more sophisticated reading. In current Native American literature, Craig Lesley finds materials that can "invite the reader as listener to become a participant in the work." Peter J. Petersen brings the study of folklore directly to the writing classroom, proposing that students provide their own materials for composition in the folk sayings and beliefs that are part of their culture. Finally, John Scally suggests that whatever one's choice of reading and writing may be, a moral dimension is both appropriate and desirable. Building on systematic steps in moral awareness, not unlike the steps in Piaget's views of language growth in children, Scally prefers truthfulness in student writing, even over clarity.

The remaining essays turn to even larger concerns that underlie the teacher's activity. Thomas C. Gorzycki calls for a humanistic response to the gloomy future of writing that is predicted in the work of Marshall McLuhan and others. David E. Jones cites Piaget and the recent work of Frank D'Angelo to justify, on solid theoretical grounds, the English teacher's concern for such traditional rhetorical modes as classification, division, and enumeration. A complementary argument by Arnold T. Orza shows the crucial function of metaphor in science, in the humanities, in all discourse. Rejecting the need for a choice between literature and composition, Orza calls for a recognition that all metaphorical language can be a source of power. Finally, Ed Hancock relates how the misuses of a particular word in high fashion academically (in this case *excellence*) can deaden the reality around it, and through semantic analysis he shows how to escape such nightmares.

As they completed this task and returned to their research and other obligations, the Fellows kindly permitted me to write an introduction to their efforts. And this is it. What we're hoping—all thirteen of us—is that this collection may provide teachers of the new students with some fresh ways of sizing up their job, and then doing it. Indeed, it's our growing conviction that much of what we have to say here about "new students," under present conditions in higher education, applies to the teaching of "old students" as well.

Walker Gibson

1 Three Ways of Looking at an Open Door

James R. Doherty
Onondaga Community College

Our seminar began with a discussion of the *Phaedrus*, Plato's discourse on love and rhetoric. At one point Socrates restates the two conditions for artful rhetoric: "First, you must know the truth about the subject that you speak or write about . . . secondly, you must have a corresponding discernment of the nature of the soul, discover the type of speech appropriate to each nature, and order and arrange your discourse accordingly." The same can be said of the teaching of reading and writing. Arguing in part from a Marxist point of view, James Doherty reverses the sequence and explores "the soul" of what some have called the "new student." This exploration leads him to a defense of a humanist education for *all* students.

We teachers have a lot of names for them, and those poured out in faculty offices are usually not complimentary, confirming that open admissions students are seldom like your old classmates. Possessing varied backgrounds and ages, they commonly lack the familiarity with written language and literature expected of college freshmen. Cross, in *Beyond the Open Door* (1971), characterizes this "new student" as scoring in the lowest third among national samples of young people on the traditional tests of academic ability. She retains this for her operational definition, but acknowledges the class, racial, and sexual bias underlying a seemingly egalitarian merit system for selecting those to be blessed with higher education. There is a high correlation between low testing and low socioeconomic status (a lovely euphemism, that); and it's difficult to get beyond high school if you're working-class, a poor tester, a woman, or nonwhite. Open admissions policy has made it easier for some of these people—at least it has opened the door. Now, what are we going to do with them?

As I see it, there are three models of remedial education. The first, and I believe the most common model, is meritocratic in philosophy and only offers a second chance for the new student to prove his or her fitness. The second is an egalitarian model which hopes to give all members of society the benefits of the traditional college education. The third model is vocational (or career oriented, to use the new terminology), offering a "New Education for New Students," the title of Cross's proposal in *Beyond the Open Door* (1971).

I want to look at all three of these models of remedial education, to help teachers decide what end they want their teaching to serve. After all, it may be that "every teacher in the community college is, in reality, a remedial teacher," as William Moore asserts.

Model 1: Panning the Silt

Teachers adhering to the first model see themselves resifting the wash that flows out of the great gold-dredging machines of the secondary schools. The theory here is clearly meritocratic: through remedial education, a select few, the flecks of gold, are saved from the mass and placed on the conveyor belts of higher education to be refined into the stuff of the elite. While his less worthy classmates are sent back where they came from, the contemporary Horatio Alger is given a helping hand on his upwardly mobile way. The emphasis is almost exclusively on access; once he's in, let's see if he can cut that same old mustard.

This burlesque of a common attitude informing English teaching in the community college results in "the open door as revolving door"—with teachers as the doormen. The concept that "some people [read "most community college students"] don't belong in college" can often be found lurking behind seemingly benign notions such as "they're not inferior, just culturally disadvantaged," or "suffering from negative self-concept," or "lacking in motivation to succeed in academic endeavors." These comfortable excuses for teachers' inability or unwillingness to help these students provide a quite practical approach. We operate a system of triage: saving the few who can rise in the meritocracy, doing little for the critically wounded beyond administering the opiate that their wounds are self-inflicted, and recommending a good graveyard for the rest. The few who are saved can make good, to the everlasting credit of the institution. No one ever hears from the others (lost as we are in the opiate we administered), and we put the least strain on our paltry resources. I find it repugnant. The battlefield and jungle metaphors aren't what I want informing my teaching.

Model 2: Molding into a Traditional Form

The crusade to give all students a full share in our cultural heritage is certainly noble. Why should those suffering from poor schooling experiences and social inequities be denied their humanity, at least as college can develop it? Only because they don't behave like the traditionally cultured? Making the new student over into the traditional student would seem to be the ultimate goal of all remedial efforts in the humanities; let's open the door of the cultural storehouse for all, not just for the elite of wealth and merit, those incestuous twins. But there are a lot of pitfalls in this model of remediation.

Overcoming Social and School Experiences

First, it's no easy job. In a good analysis of the failings of this model, Cross (1971) goes so far as to claim that "new students are not the same shape as traditional students" (p. 158). Two patterns of social and school experience feed upon themselves, making it impossible for many of these students to succeed in school without a reorientation to learning. In an article focused on a primary concern —language development—Deutsch (1965) explains how a teacher-perceived deficiency in language functioning due to class origin becomes increasingly pronounced with each year in school. This cumulative deficit causes school to lose much of its intended socializing and learning effect because language is central to the school experience, both for abstracting into manipulative symbols and for asserting membership in a community of learners.

A student's awareness of a personal inability to perform the linguistic tasks expected by the teacher, and of the attention lavished on the few who can, reinforces a sense of low status. This leads to a reticence toward communicating across the class lines that are drawn early and often in the classroom. Out goes functional motivation to perform linguistically in anything but peer interaction. The most distressing aspect of the cumulative deficit hypothesis is that it becomes progressively more difficult to reverse.

Bruner also emphasizes the central importance of language to formal education in *Toward a Theory of Instruction* (1966), echoing two Soviet experiments which found that "language, in short, provides an internal technique for programming our discriminations, our behaviour, our forms of awareness. If there is suitable internal language, the task can be done" (pp. 108–109). So without "suitable internal language" the learning activities would appear to be hopeless and very threatening to a student's integrity, given the student competition in most classrooms. Then we have what Bruner (1966) calls "defending" rather than "coping." "Coping respects the requirements of problems we encounter while still respecting our integrity. . . . Defending is a strategy whose objective is avoiding or escaping from problems for which we believe there is no solution that does not violate our integrity of functioning" (p. 129).

Bruner sees learning blocks as defenses against the activity of learning itself. Such activity threatens the students' sense of themselves, so they focus on protecting themselves from the dangerous situation. Bruner believes school depends on denaturing or delibidinizing learning, freeing the intellectual activity from its affective links. For the new student this may not have happened. These new students—working-class, women, and minorities for the most part— have experienced school as a series of constant attacks on their worth. School may be so threatening to their integrity that they "miss out on a good deal of what is going on because they have such an absorbing investment in scanning the world [here, of the classroom] for danger" (Bruner, 1966, p. 142).

So we have the threat-of-failure syndrome which Holt details in his engaging *How Children Fail* (1970):

> Until recently it had not occurred to me that poor students thought differently about their work than good students; I assumed they thought the same way, only less skillfully. Now it looks as if the expectations and fear of failure, if stong enough, may lead children to act and think in a special way, to adopt strategies different from those of more confident children. (p. 48)

Of course Holt, Bruner, and Deutsch are discussing preadolescent children, but Cross deduces this same syndrome from her data on the new student. She found a lack of self-confidence in school situations; nervousness and tension in class, often paralyzing in their intensity; and a defeatist attitude. The expectation of failure is so great that many students quickly cease trying, believing you can't lose when you haven't made any bets. In light of the cumulative nature of the problem, we college teachers are probably seeing the wound at a more advanced stage, after years of festering.

Because these students react differently to learning activities does not mean that they cannot be freed from the "pre-emptive metaphors," as Bruner calls them. He maintains that learning is almost involuntary, the human specialization. Can we expect intellectual growth in a new student equal to that of the old student, once the will to learn is freed from its "mind-forg'd manacles"? Mina Shaughnessy (1976), the guru of basic writing, believes so. In Bruner's work and in John Carroll's "A Model for School Learning" she finds evidence that, given sufficient time and adequate instruction, everyone, excepting the severely handicapped, can learn any subject or master any skill no matter how complex or subtle, although there may be differences in ways and rate of learning; aptitude is only a measure of time. I'm not so sure. Is it possible to reorient these students to learning, as Bruner and Cross call for, given the competitive, class-ridden educational system? Perhaps it's not the students who need to be reoriented.

Overcoming Anti-intellectualism

But apparently that's not the only way in which students differ from teachers. Cross's research (1971) also convinces her that they are career-oriented to the point of being anti-intellectual, and "pragmatic seekers of immediate and tangible rewards"; that they spend all their leisure watching television, fixing cars, or sewing clothes; and that they are nonquestioning authoritarians by principle and personality. Remember, this is no deficiency conception—Cross would never call "them" inferior, just different. What it comes down to, in her analysis, is that all the stereotypes are true. We might have known—there's "them" and there's "us."

In addition, the career goals of the second model are unrealizable. The monetary value of any college degree is in direct relation to its scarcity. When 80 percent of the population have a college degree it will be worth no more than the high school degree, significant only when missing. The world won't rearrange itself to fit the expectations of the new graduate, and that world expects that in 1980 only 20 percent of its jobs will require college-trained workers. Sennett and Cobb (1973), referring to Ivar Berg's *Education and Jobs: The Great Training Robbery*, maintain that the real skill requirements for most jobs have not increased in the last three decades. Automation and the growth of technological industries are not replacing low-skill routine jobs with more intellectually taxing work that demands higher levels of education. One set of low-level jobs is simply replaced by a different set; or, even worse, expertise is concentrated in fewer workers, causing an overall decrease in the demand for skilled human labor. Getting through college en masse will not help the new students vocationally; employers will simply raise the educational requirements for menial work. In a stratified society the bottom third will still be the bottom third, although the means for maintaining rank may change.

Model 3: Educating for the World of Work

The third remedial model is now called "career education" (known as "vocational education" in the good old days before doublespeak was carried to such heights). This model seems to be waxing as the second model wanes. Karabel (1972) reported that 30 percent of community college students were in vocational courses. Grubb and Lazerson (1975), in their excellent essay on career education, claimed a consensus that the figure was then about 50 percent.

Community college teachers know too well the growth of so-called career programs at the expense of liberal arts courses. The idea is to educate people with their future place in the world of work (and, by the way, in the social order) in mind. John Gardner (1961), that incompetent philosopher, writes that "An excellent plumber is infinitely more admirable than an incompetent philosopher." Cross (1971) rejoices that "Colleges can be different and excellent too" (or is it "separate but equal," "equity not equality," or "some of my best friends are new students"?). This will lead us to courses in "Writing for Plumbers" and "Pipes and Poems: Plumbing the Depths of Literature." Education for the new student will be aimed at "reducing expectations, limiting aspirations, and increasing commitments to the existing social structure"—that is, cooling them out.

Maybe Simone de Beauvoir (1974) can help us here, although admittedly in a different context:

> At most they were willing to grant "equity in difference" to the *other* sex. That profitable formula is most significant; it is precisely like the "equal but separate" formula of the Jim Crow laws aimed at the North American Negroes. As is well known, this so-called equalitarian segregation has resulted only in the most extreme discrimination. The similarity just noted is in no way due to chance, for whether it is a race, a caste, a class, or a sex that is reduced to a position of inferiority, the methods of justification are the same, "the eternal feminine" corresponds to "the black souls" and to "the Jewish character." . . . Both are being emancipated today from a like paternalism, and the former master class wishes to "keep them in their places"—that is, the place chosen for them. In both cases the former masters lavish more or less sincere eulogies,

either on the virtues of "the good Negro" with his dormant, child-ish, merry soul—the submissive Negro—or on the merits of the woman who is "truly feminine"—that is, frivolous, infantile, irre-sponsible—the submissive woman. In both cases the dominant class bases its argument on a state of affairs that it has itself created. As George Bernard Shaw puts it, in substance, "The American white relegates the black to the rank of shoeshine boy: and he concludes from this that the black is good for nothing but shining shoes." This vicious circle is met with in all analogous circum-stances; when an individual (or a group of individuals) is kept in a situation of inferiority, the fact is that he is inferior. But the signif-icance of the verb *to be* must be rightly understood here; it is in bad faith to give it a static value when it really has the dynamic Hegelian sense of "to have become." Yes, women on the whole *are* today inferior to men; that is, their situation affords them fewer possibilities. The question is: should that state of affairs continue? (pp. xxvii–xxviii)

Vocationalism has been with us since the 1880s, when it was pushed to increase economic productivity and limit social decay by eradicating poverty, alienation, social unrest, and dropping out. Oddly, we still have all those problems. Vocational education didn't help the problems, nor did it help the students. About all it did was to reinforce racial, class, and sexual bias and to make certain that those new students, immigrants and migrating blacks, knew they were second-class. Here we are in the 1970s with the big lie of American egalitarianism encouraging everyone to seek a college education, with already too many underemployed college graduates, with high job dissatisfaction and worker unrest, with a literal army of angry and cynical Vietnam veterans, and having just passed through a crisis of racial and student unrest. Career education to the rescue. Grubb and Lazerson (1975) observe that

vocationalism has been consistently offered as a general solution: it promised to integrate working-class and immigrant children into the high school and to solve the labor conflicts in the late nine-teenth and early twentieth centuries; it promised to solve the prob-lems of technological unemployment and the lack of opportunity for minorities during the 1960's; and career education promises to solve the problems of over-educated and under-educated youth, restore the fit between schooling and work, and reverse the increas-ing disaffection with the schools.

The advantages may be manifold: the value of the elite degrees won't be undermined; perhaps the mass would be better adjusted, or to put it another way, would know their place; and it's a lot easier to teach minimum vocational literacy than full participation in human culture. That is, if it worked. Might a century of failure to hide basic social contradictions be ended with a magical name change? That woman who graduated from New Bedford Vocational School in home economics because her junior high counselor said that was where she belonged is going to be so much happier and more productive with her A.A.S. in child care. Now she can make the minimum wage while changing diapers in an orphanage, rather than emptying bedpans in a nursing home. Don't listen to the malcontent who yells from the back row, "It's easy enough for John Gardner and K. Patricia Cross to recommend that—their kids aren't going to be new students." Cross even says that we'll overthrow status distinctions just so this plan can work.

Evaluating Our Perceptions of Social Class

Before we go any further, let's ask: What makes "an excellent plumber"? Are people only their jobs? Shouldn't we work for the day when every plumber is a humane man of letters, a competent philosopher? Are the plumber and the philosopher creatures of different species, evolved to fit the division of labor? Just how different are the new students?

These questions resemble those underlying Sennett and Cobb's *The Hidden Injuries of Class* (1973). Are there a few elite people— "us"—who are concerned with matters of cultural and philosophical import, who desire to rise above simple materialistic concerns, while the mass—"them"—are pragmatic, career-oriented hedonists, seeing heaven in a Sears catalog? Is it true, and always to be true, that "culture and the masses, if not necessarily enemies, have at best few interests in common"? (p. 6) Is "man lives not by bread alone" a truism only for an elite with an aptitude for culture?

What of the anti-intellectualism that Cross sees as preventing the new student from succeeding in a traditional liberal arts education? Sennett and Cobb (1973) discovered an astounding reverence for education and culture among the workers they interviewed in Boston. They found a deep-seated belief "that high culture permits a life in which material need can be transcended by a higher form of self-control" (p. 23). These struggling workers insisted that their children receive more education than they themselves had because they saw education as an "escape from becoming creatures of circumstance, more chance to develop the defenses, the tools of personal rational control" (p. 25).

But this is not some simple peasant faith in the virtues of their masters. They have seen how education works in practice, besides sensing its potential. They have seen the educated twist their advantages into an opportunity to contribute less to the communal welfare while appropriating more of its benefits. They have felt the power of the institutions of school and work as they insisted on their inadequacy, throwing their class in their faces at every turn. They resent this exploitation and these attacks on their integrity, and this hostility combines with a loyalty to their comrades, making a complex ambivalence toward education. While desiring the virtues that education might bring, these workers are unwilling to sacrifice their principles of class loyalty to personal distinction.

The "pragmatic seekers of immediate and tangible rewards," when interviewed at length, reveal that their desire for a car, a house, and the ever escalating ante of consumer goods is not at all a desire for creature comforts; it is the expression of a need to affirm their personal worth and their power to shape their environment. Sennett and Cobb (1973) describe a Greek immigrant who worked as a janitor, slaving to buy a home, not for comfort, but for "a sanctuary, a living space . . . where he would not find his place in society thrown in his face over the smallest matters" (p. 48). In 1972 he earned $10,000, owned a home, drove a car, had money in the bank for his children's education; yet, he felt "vulnerable and inadequately armed, but what has he done wrong?" (p. 50)

These are not some alien "them." They need a humanistic education for the same reasons we do—to make sense of their lives—and if that sense cannot be made, they need to do something about it. As an Australian visitor to our seminar said, we need to "maintain the integrity of their stupidity."

Questioning Our Teaching Goals

Questions about standards must always be answered in light of teachers' hopes for their students. If they are only interested in helping a mechanic write a parts order or read a repair manual, humanistic consciousness-raising is clearly out of place. But if freeing thwarted students to realize their possibilities is the teacher's goal, rhetorical norms or standards will be of secondary concern. The controversy over "the students' right to their own language" cannot be resolved by considering only the linguistic equality of dialects. If the goal is to help Horatio Alger on his way, fit him out with a banker's dialect along with the pin-striped suit.

What about the "back-to-basics movement" which seems not so

strangely coincidental with the career education push? Doesn't the definition of *basics* depend on the purpose of the education? Does technical writing make any sense without an endorsement of career education? These root questions have to carry over into literature courses as well. If you're going to advocate teaching popular literature rather than Shakespeare in the one literature course available to many community college students, are you trying to reorient your students to the possibilities of literature, or are you only extending a disguised tracking system, locking the students into place? Shall we continue the college preparatory business, and general education system that victimized so many of our students in high school; or shall we try, impossible as the job may be, to overcome the discrimination so inherent in our educational and social system?

I don't want to integrate people into an economic and social order that wastes their possibilities. If developing their capabilities puts them in traumatic conflict with the expectations of the political economy, so be it. Perhaps we can resolve the conflict in such a way that the full development of every citizen becomes the *raison d'etre* for the social order. Rather than lowering our educational goals, and the students' aspirations, we should rearrange the world to fit the needs of the students. This contradiction between the goals of education and the needs of its master, the political economy, makes futile any hope for a fourth model, a best of all possible compromises for this best of all possible worlds. As teachers, we will always come back to the same question: Are we educating people, or plumbers, or only prospecting for the ruling class?

2 "Scientism" and the Teaching of English

James J. Kinney
Virginia Commonwealth University

The preceding essay makes the point that the new students are not statistical constructs but human beings. Defining their needs implies certain political decisions, ones we teachers might prefer to avoid. But we do make these decisions, and the way in which we decide determines whether we dehumanize our students and, in so doing, dehumanize ourselves. In the following essay, James Kinney is also concerned with dehumanizing decisions, but shifts our attention from the students to the subject taught. He warns against choosing "scientism" as a basic approach to teaching English.

Science and humanism are not opposites. We are not forced into an either/or choice between them. In their highest forms they actually merge and give the world an Einstein or a Schweitzer. But the twentieth century seems to have posited science and humanism as opposites—industrialization, technological warfare, atomic holocaust on one hand, art, music, poetry on the other. We in the humanities have ourselves been prone to dividing the world into "us" and "them," but with a curious result. While believing in the science/humanism dichotomy and proclaiming the superiority of the humanities, we have belied our claims by flattering science through imitation. We seem to have bought the idea that not to be scientific is to be irrational. For the last fifty years, for example, literary criticism has been progressively refining itself into an imitation of scientific method. Now the teaching of writing seems to face an either/or choice—to pursue either a scientific approach or an irrational one. If we are to avoid mistakes of the past, writing teachers today need reassurance that the dichotomy, and the choice, are false.

11

SOUTHERN BAPTIST COLLEGE LIBRARY

The Real Dichotomy

In *Modern Dogma and the Rhetoric of Assent* (1974), Booth explains the real dichotomy, which is not between science and humanism but between "scientism" and "irrationalism." According to Booth, this dualism began with Descartes' separation of mind and matter. When empirical science later demonstrated such mastery of the material universe, the concept of "scientism" emerged. This reverence for the empirically verifiable, exemplified by the logical positivists, contrasted with the "irrational" world of human values. Value judgments were not subject to empirical analysis and validation, and hence were ultimately absurd. Booth, in his best Aristotelian manner, is seeking the *via media*, a balanced view of reason's place in the affairs of humanity. But his plea is for the future; the dichotomy Booth rejects is still with us. We are still given to scientismic awe for scientific appearances. I believe this scientismic attitude has long been apparent in our profession's dominant view of what literary criticism should be. As attention shifts from literature to writing, that long-neglected stepchild, I fear the same scientismic attitude may come to dominate again.

Many of us have sensed a kind of erosion in the humanities and blamed it on a dichotomy between science and humanism. As science moved from one triumph to another in our century, from Kitty Hawk to the moon, the humanities lost their central role in education and in life. Money and status flowed to the sciences in the world and in academe. But this apparent triumph of science over rival fields was not in itself harmful, because science and humanism are complementary, not competitive. "They" could never defeat "us." Only we could defeat ourselves.

As we watched the sciences move into new buildings while English departments huddled in the old, we began to create our own problems. We wanted to get on the bandwagon. Soon every discipline strove to be an "-ology" in the restricted sense of "the science of." Emphasis on empirical procedures, collection of data, and formulation of "laws" spread into every field. The result wasn't that we became scientists or that we competed with the sciences but that we infected our own disciplines with a false dichotomy between scientism and irrationalism.

Actually, the new sense of tough-minded objectivity had many positive effects at first, draining the swamps in which many had been mired. In psychology, for example, John Watson's behaviorism was a beneficial move out of the long, sterile maunderings of the introspectionists. But psychologists, seeing an either/or choice between scientism and irrationalism, chose scientism and gave the world B. F. Skinner in all his glory. English teachers have been smugly aware of the psychologists' folly, and smugly aware that colleagues in education, sociology, and political science have stooped to similar folly—pursuing scientism into ever deeper quagmires of data collection and jargon. But English departments, more often than not, have been equally guilty of pursuing scientism; the old houses we have huddled in have been mostly made of glass.

The Ascent of Modernism

Earlier in this century the loss of religious faith and the apparent triumph of science drove humanists to take shelter in existentialism. But belief in a humanly absurd, irrational universe created the doctrine of Modernism, which has dominated aesthetic thought for decades. In brief, the humanist turned away from the chaos and absurdity of the universe at large, to find solace in the reason and order of man's created universe of art. The Modernist aesthetic led to viewing a work of art as an object, as an ordered structure of parts, and thus to an emphasis on form.

Development of New Criticism

In literary criticism, of course, this meant New Criticism. Again, the first effects were positive. New Criticism, as one professor commented, taught many people how to read. But teachers of literature, no less than those in other fields, became obsessed with objectivity and scientific precision. They soon cleared away the nineteenth-century swamp with a vengeance. *Romanticism* and *subjectivity* became the foulest of dirty words. As Ohmann has pointed out (1976, pp. 242-52), a bifurcated English department developed. Our *raison d'etre* to the outside world was the service provided by teaching composition, but our self-value lay in our "disciplined" approach to literature, a now-objectified "field" to be categorized and analyzed like any other. At first New Criticism—and later, formalism—held sway only at elitist schools. But by the 1960s the doctrines and terminology were omnipresent, and by 1963, Northrop Frye, in an essay for new graduate students in English, could assert that their lives as scholarly critics would be devoted to classifying genres and describing literary structures. Once formalism became *the* mode for training all literature teachers, the either/or choice had been made for the English profession—we, too, had chosen scientism.

With the choice made, certain results seemed to flow inevitably, especially once the vestiges of opposition were swept away. While all graduate programs were being brought into line, a similar unification of approach was taking place vertically. Applebee (1974, pp. 185–215) relates how the Basic Issues Conference in 1958 led to the end of "progressivism" in elementary and secondary English programs. Emphasis on the subjective needs of the child was replaced by the "academic liberal" approach, with a curriculum logically organized according to the structure of the discipline. With the profession solidly organized and solidly committed to scientism, the question became: How scientific can we be in English? The answer, of course, was our blossoming love affair with linguistics.

Recruitment of Structural Linguistics

Structural linguistics had been around for some time before the sixties, but our search for the ultimate in a scientific approach to language and literature took off just as transformational-generative grammar (TGG) came on the scene. No subjective nonsense here! The leading theorists in TGG came from backgrounds in physics, mathematics, and symbolic logic; the foremost spokesman taught at Massachusetts Institute of Technology. Structural grammar, however, did not lose out completely. In a circuitous route similar to Poe's influence on Imagist poetry, structural linguistics had influenced the work of French anthropologist Claude Lévi-Strauss, whose structural anthropology in turn influenced French literary critics such as Roland Barthes. Soon French structuralist criticism was all the rage in American graduate schools. This newest criticism is much more scientific than the old New Criticism, which still involved syntagmatic—in effect, chronological—analysis. Now one could do paradigmatic analysis, breaking the literary work down into structural patterns arranged in paradigms. Structural criticism now includes concepts taken from TGG and is already spreading downward from graduate centers to general classroom teachers. Steinley (1976) points with pride to the accomplishments of Gerald Prince's "narratology" in reducing narrative art to "phrase structure rules," such as:

$$M\ St\ ----------\!\!\to E + CCL + E + CCL + E$$

and,

$$E \longrightarrow \begin{cases} \text{E stat} \ / \ \# \text{ ---} \\ \text{E stat} \ / \text{ --- } \# \\ \text{E act} \end{cases} \qquad \text{(p. 313)}$$

Effect of Scientism on Humanities

I began by implying that the choice, and pursuit, of scientism has been a primrose path for our literary colleagues. We have all bemoaned the drastic reduction in number of English majors in recent years, despite the fact that there are more students in college today than ever before. We have explained that decline repeatedly in terms of contemporary economic, political, and social factors. With not a scintilla of supporting data, I submit that, more than any other factor, our choice of scientism has led to our decline. Again, it is not that the humanities and sciences are in opposition, but rather that the humanities once offered an alternative way of learning about and experiencing the world—not a better way or a worse way, just a different way. Students once came to us for that alternative. But in pursuing a formalistic approach to teaching literature, we achieved Ortega y Gasset's goal of dehumanizing art. Dehumanized humanities have nothing to offer our human students. If they want formulas they can go to physics and get better, more productive ones; there the formulas can take people to the moon and machines to the stars. Our formulas have done nothing but deaden the souls of young people who came to us eager to explore the mysterious universe within.

The end, in a whimper, of literary studies may yet be averted. The outbreak of irrationalism in the late sixties was a powerful statement of student dissatisfaction with the scientism that dominated academe, and the results have not been all bad. Interest in subjective criticism is growing, for example, in the work of Barrett Mandel, Stanley Fish, and David Bleich. More important, the widespread interest in rhetorical criticism holds much hope because this approach emphasizes the human relationship between author and audience instead of the scientific relationship of observer and object. But, while the pendulum may have begun to swing back in literary studies, the recent focus on composition may throw writing instruction, after years of benign neglect, directly into the tempting embrace of scientism.

Prognosis for Composition

Just as the earlier introduction of objective approaches had an initially salutary effect on psychology, the current excitement in rhetoric and composition owes much to the sweeping away of stagnant, unexamined attitudes. In the 1880s, Barrett Wendell institutionalized freshman composition as a new course at Harvard University. Despite the general semantics and "communication" fads of the 1940s and '50s, there was not much change until the 1960s. We know the chaos that has reigned since then, especially the battles between the "uptaught" and the "hang loose" schools, as Edward P. J. Corbett once called them.

Concurrently, objective knowledge from behavioral and cognitive psychology and from linguistics has been brought to bear on the writing process, stimulating new theories and much discussion of what had been for most college professors a moribund subject. So far, so good; but the path to a neosterility—this time hidden behind a rich foliage of statistical analyses, laboratory experiments, and jargon—would be very easy to follow. Already the influence of behavioral psychology has been immense at the community college level. Many of us teachers have resisted behaviorism for two reasons: first, it is openly hostile to the kind of values, such as human freedom and dignity, we proclaim, and second, it has been forced on us from outside—it is the educationist's scientism, not ours. But scientism it is, and in the form of objectives, programmed texts, and packaged "learning experiences," it has claimed a solid piece of the writing instruction territory, particularly in basic writing courses. No doubt, the back-to-basics movement will give further impetus to behavioral approaches.

As humanists, our response to behaviorism has been to increase the tempo of our own development as "scientists exploring writing technology," largely by turning to the more compatible theories of cognitive psychology and linguistics. Cognitive psychology, particularly the work of Vygotsky, Piaget, and Bruner, has provided a developmental theory of language acquisition, beginning with innate structuring principles universally present in the human mind. In *Teaching the Universe of Discourse* (1968), Moffett has systematically applied aspects of cognitive theory to writing instruction. D'Angelo's *A Conceptual Theory of Rhetoric* (1975) has aroused considerable interest, and he too relies on cognitive psychology, suggesting that it provides a scientific base for teaching the traditional modes of organizing exposition, but for teaching them as heuristics because these patterns actually correspond to innate structures of the mind.

Not long ago, however, scientism reared its head when Lauer (1970) gave us pages of bibliography on psychology and flatly stated that we cannot have a heuristic for rhetoric without relying on the scientists to provide it for us. Berthoff (1971) responded with a cogent analysis of the dangers inherent in Lauer's position, but the cognitive psychology bandwagon has been gathering speed.

The problem, of course, is not with reaching out to science for whatever there is that may be of use to us. Rather, the problem is the belief that there is a dichotomy, and that we are on the weak side of it. Cognitive psychology is not ahead of us in providing a heuristic for rhetoric; it is just now beginning to gather bits and pieces of empirical data to support the heuristics we have long had. As D'Angelo indicates, Aristotle presented us with classification and division, comparison and contrast, as ways of exploring a subject. It is gratifying to learn that Piaget and Bruner are now establishing experimental verification, but let's keep the cart before the horse. We have, in fact, in Elbow's *Writing without Teachers* (1973), a near-perfect discovery procedure for rhetoric. That no psychologist can yet explain in empirical terminology why or how Elbow's method works is surely no reason to reject it, not unless one has thoroughly dichotomized the world and decided that truth can only be found in scientism. Certainly, explorations of other fields can be useful and stimulating, certainly students of writing instruction should be intimately familiar with work such as Moffett's and D'Angelo's, or even directly with that of Piaget or Bruner; but as programs to train writing teachers develop, we must be aware of the self-destructive implications represented by scientism such as Lauer's.

The New Grammar and Composition

Closely related to our growing interest in cognitive psychology has been our general enthusiasm for linguistics. In particular, the study of style has benefited from the objective methodologies provided by transformational-generative grammar, as Winterowd asserted in *Rhetoric: A Synthesis* (1968, pp. 103–111). Perhaps more than anyone else, Winterowd has been associated with the application of TGG, and more recently of Fillmore's "case grammar," to a theory of composition. He is also directing the nation's first Ph.D. program fully devoted to rhetoric and composition. Winterowd himself presents a balanced view of the contribution new grammars may make to the teaching of writing. He states in *Contemporary Rhetoric* that "we now have a useful and productive 'technology' for teaching sentence structure." But then he asks the really important question, "Should we or should we not run students through a series of exercises designed to activate their [syntactic] competence?" He concludes that hermetically sealed exercises can have only "a tangential relationship to the real use of language," that "systematic exercises have no place in the composition class," that the teaching of sentence structure should have "all the glorious and productive *lack of system* that characterizes most real language learning tasks" (p. 254).

This is a marvelously humanistic view and one that Winterowd maintains throughout his work. Even so, the insidious lure of scientism seems to touch him at times. Consider his statement in "Linguistics and Composition," addressed to composition teachers: "We need to understand the theory [of TGG] in general, but we are not obliged to remain at the cutting edge of the field or to follow the detailed arguments of *linguists who are attempting to bring their instrument, the grammar, to perfection* in any of its parts" (p. 201, italics added). The first half of the statement exemplifies the balance Winterowd brings to the subject, but the second half hints of scientism, implying that linguists are going to arrive at "perfection," that we writing teachers are following their lead to some ultimate, empirical truth. Moreover, TGG is named an "instrument," suggesting all the concrete, useful connotations of that term, reifying a purely theoretical construct.

Winterowd is well versed in linguistics and consciously seeks a balanced view of that subject's relationship to composition. How much more easily those of us who are not so knowledgeable in linguistics can be tainted with scientism when we look at all those tree diagrams, phonological matrices, and impressive rewrite rules. We struggle to teach writing, we operate in darkness and in doubt, and we are twentieth-century persons imbued with awe for science. Scientists of language seem to hold the last best hope for our salvation, and we all too willingly succumb to the spell.

Tagmemic Theory of Composition

One cannot discuss scientism and the teaching of writing without mentioning another linguistic theory—tagmemics—and the work of

Young, Becker, and Pike (1970). Just as TGG gives us some useful ways of looking at the structure of sentences, tagmemic theory offers insight into the structure of units larger than the sentence, especially the paragraph. Both TGG and tagmemics are helpful in post-facto description of writing, and thus have something to offer at the late or editorial stages of the writing process. But Young, Becker, and Pike have chosen to emphasize tagmemic theory as a heuristic procedure in the initial or discovery stage of the process, and have borrowed the terms "particle, wave, and field" from physics to describe this heuristic. Their system for varying one's point of view on a subject obviously has some merit, but I suspect we may be falling prey to scientism if we accept its elegant design and scientific terminology as proof that it is *the* heuristic, our own answer to scientific method.

As rhetoricians, I think we should be more sensitive to the persuasive implications of the scientific terminology. Particle, wave, and field immediately bring to mind the awe-inspiring successes of quantum physics—who dares question? In any event, while I respect many of those who acclaim particle, wave, and field as *the* heuristic, I submit that we might do better to take it with a grain of salt. I keep remembering Corder's comments in an article called "What I Learned at School" (1975), where he says:

> We hungered after various heuristic models for discovery; we looked at this, that and the other thing as particles, waves, and fields. We even tried the TUTO rhythmic method (and I'll be glad to answer letters inquiring after the TUTO mysteries). But the sorry truth is . . . I was never able to try portions of the essays from different perspectives . . . to take a possible subject, hold it in my hand, look at it this way and that way, and scout its possibilities. (p. 331)

Corder's experience matches my own, and I simply wonder how many of us, or how many of our students, truly find a scientific heuristic all that productive. In fact, it often seems that the more scientific and systematized the heuristic, the more it is apt to produce the kind of mechanical writing Kenneth Macrorie calls "Engfish" and William Coles refers to as "themewriting." Emig (1964) pointed out that the more "conscious" the writing process, the more "conscious," i.e., labored, the result. Actually, a heuristic need not be methodical at all; fundamentally, a heuristic is anything that generates investigation and discovery. A simple proposition can be a powerful heuristic if offered as a premise around which thought may be structured. For example, try offering as a basic premise the proposition that men are more intelligent than women at the next faculty discussion of pay increases.

Need for Moderation in Viewing Scientism

Warnock (1976a) correctly cautions against being "afraid of theory," and I want to guard against my being misinterpreted. I truly appreciate theoretical advance and enjoyed Warnock's own such offerings. I am simply suggesting that we not be steamrollered in our theoretical orientation into a one-dimensional, scientismic posture. People talk about making a bridge between science and the humanities, but the traffic seems to be all one way. Imports are brought back from forays into the sciences and we shove aside much that is of value in our own heritage. I suspect, for example, that in our enthusiasm for particle, wave, and field theory, we may be neglecting the full potential of such nonscientismic heuristics as Kenneth Burke's pentad of act, agent, agency, scene, and purpose. This heuristic derives from a study of drama and focuses on the human element in a subject rather than on its "thingness."

Another valuable discovery procedure originates in a concern with the mysterious aspects of human creativity, rather than in the empirically identifiable stages of so-called problem solving. Rohman and Wlecke (Rohman, 1965; Rohman & Wlecke, 1964) have given us a very humanistic, rational approach to invention in their work on what has come to be called pre-writing. Their discussions of journal-keeping and meditative techniques have been neglected in our search for structure and precision in discovery procedures.

In sum, we certainly should not be afraid of either science or theory. We would do well, however, to be leery of our lack of confidence which tends to make us feel inferior because we are not scientists ourselves.

Linguistic Theory and Practical Application

Actual scientists find our attempts to co-opt science rather confusing at times, if not downright amusing. For example, few people trained purely in linguistics have any interest in connecting their work with writing instruction and don't seem to understand rhetoricians' obsessive insistence that there is a connection. Most linguists, except for dialecticians, are quick to explain that they are only concerned with "competence" (the theoretical construct that says all human beings come equipped with the capacity to develop the whole structure of a language) and not with linguistic "performance" (how people actually use a language). Grammatical theory—TGG, for example—can provide phrase structure and transformational rules which accurately account for the production of all English sentences that are grammatical and which generate none that are not. But this fact does not mean that the mind actually uses those rules and transformations in either producing or processing sentences. Linguists are the first to state that there is no necessary connection between their theoretical work and the way people use language in everyday communication. As Chomsky says in the classic *Language and Mind*:

> We noted at the outset that performance and competence must be sharply distinguished if either is to studied successfully. We have now discovered a certain model of competence. It would be tempting, but quite absurd, to regard it as a model of performance as well. Thus we might propose that to produce a sentence, the speaker goes through the successive steps of constructing a base-derivation, line by line from the initial symbol S, then inserting lexical items and applying grammatical transformations to form a surface structure, and finally applying the phonological rules in their given order, in accordance with the cyclic principle discussed earlier. There is not the slightest justification for any such assumption. (p. 157).

To better understand what Chomsky means, we might look at linguistic rules as analogous to the "laws" of physics and at linguists as theoretical physicists. Physics applied to the external world can accomplish marvelous things, but it can tell us little about the psychomotor behavior of a human being, except to describe its effects. Physical laws can describe and predict the flight of a handball as it is hit and caroms off walls, ceiling, and floor. But physics cannot explain what goes on inside the mind of an experienced handball player that allows him or her to know, at the instant the ball is hit, where to move to meet it. The psychological processes involved are unobservable and unrelated to physical laws and mathematical formulas. The psychological processes involved in producing language are about equally unobservable, despite the best efforts of psycholinguists to study them.

Actually, the pure linguist, like the physicist, is not basically concerned with the processes themselves, but only with creating formulas adequate for describing the effects. Moreover, neither the theory of the physicist nor the theory of the linguist is "true"; we know, for example, that Newtonian laws operate only within certain limits. These theories are mental constructs, nothing more. They are convenient ways of describing something that has been observed. They are simply devices, to use Owen Barfield's phrase, for "saving the appearances."

Scientists themselves know these limitations and are refreshingly honest about them. The best illustration of the limits of linguistics as a science is an anecdote related to me by a young instructor of linguistics at the University of Massachusetts. He compared the scientist studying language today with a man who studied a Coke machine. Every day the man spent hours in observing as person after person walked up, deposited a quarter, and waited until the machine coughed forth a shiny red can of Coke. Intrigued, the observer puzzled over this phenomenon at great length and finally constructed a theory to describe how it worked. He rushed to his workshop and soon produced a beautiful working model that looked just like the Coke machine and duplicated its functioning right down to the soft "plop" as the can came out. One day, however, he suffered a fatal shock. He was again observing the original machine when, for the first time, a Coke truck pulled up. The driver opened the machine, took out the collected quarters, and filled the interior racks with shiny red cans of Coke. Our observer, of course, had built a machine that took in the quarter, flattened it, rolled it into the size and shape of a can, and painted it bright red.

The Risk in Adopting Scientism

The problem is not in our scientists, it is in ourselves. We want too much to believe that there is an answer to all the problems of teaching composition, and, wanting that, we are too eager to see science as the redeemer. We might be more objective about our problems if we saw them as parallel to those faced by our colleagues who are teaching music and art. Most of us would find it amusing to watch them scramble all over optical and acoustical physics in an attempt to learn how to teach basic drawing or piano. If we are not careful, someone will fill our need to believe, but it won't be the scientists; it will be the scientismic members of our own profession, especially those in the graduate programs of prestige institutions. The fine minds working in our most renowned graduate centers have devoted years to making the study of literature as scientismic a pursuit as possible, and we have seen the gospel according to Harvard, Yale, Berkeley, and Hopkins spread down the academic pyramid.

So far, these worthies have regarded composition and rhetoric as inferior, methodological rather than substantive subjects. But if, as seems likely, the academic study of literature diminishes to an occupational status about on a par with the study of classics, then other name-brand institutions will follow the lead of Iowa, Michigan, Southern California, and Ohio State into the writing business. In that event, as now, the law of academic downward mobility will govern. The danger is that scientism may govern with it, for scientism could quickly come to dominate the teaching of composition. Picture an item in the *MLA Job List*: "Beginning Assistant Professor. Dissertation in tagmemic heuristics, to teach three comp sections and possible upper division class in specialty. Ph.D. required, publications desirable." Dozens of sweaty-palmed neophytes who fit that job description will wander hotel hallways, waiting for the chance to become the "heuristics person" at some tiny college. And students will wander college hallways, driven from scientismic writing classes just as they were driven from literature.

3 What *Am* I Teaching?

Theresa L. Enroth
American River College

Some community college students do not resemble those described by James Doherty. Their parents have gone to college, and they too have always expected to go. However, they have had little interest in English in school and have learned nothing about the humanities. Distracted by television, these students are impatient with books. At the California community college where Theresa Enroth teaches, second-semester freshman English provides an introduction to drama, poetry, and fiction. Since it is not required for the Associate in Arts degree nor for transfer to most universities, the course is elected by only the fairly capable students who have known some academic success. But even they have little experience of literature and are puzzled, perhaps even anxious, when they confront it in the classroom.

I am a tough-minded, no-nonsense teacher of literature and composition—of the timeless works of the imagination and of clear, logical exposition. I am an open-minded liberal: I would never indoctrinate my students. I would defend to their deaths their right to resist, challenge, and disagree (in logical, clear prose). I believe the world can be set to rights with language. I am also a sensitive soul who knows that deep in the hearts of even the most inarticulate student lies poetry. I teach my students about the beauty and symmetry of the pre-Copernican universe. I impress them with the absurdity and indifference of the world. I slip from the chain of being one week into existentialism the next, displaying utter conviction. In short, I am a schizoid, a phony, and a liar.

I am also given to overstatement. But my students, too, are extremists. They believe that I believe the substance of whatever literature I teach. No disclaimer will rescue me from their conviction that the content of our literature represents my views. For them, response to ideas and themes in what we read is immediate

25

and honest. They assume it is the same for me, and whether or not I mean to proselytize, I do.

Knowing this, I must confront the possibility that implicit in every choice of poem, essay, or story is an effort to influence the students' views. Even while I try to center discussion on structure or device, I am promoting a world view. I am inculcating what I conceive to be civilization. Like the statues in E. E. Cummings's park, my choices of specific examples loom solidly as delinations of my own values and convictions.

Content as a Factor

I do not believe I am alone in my failure to confront the implications of content. Many English teachers, preoccupied with genre and style, avoid these troublesome implications. And we miss, at the same time, the simplest and strongest method of interesting our students in reading. In our own bloodless world of form, everything, as Arnheim (1966) says, seems to count except the subject of the work. But for students, form is only a hazy concept; their primary interest is in the subject, and their secondary interest often is in the teacher's attitude toward the subject. They haven't learned to command the critical stance that enables us to escape the "compelling call of art." Students associate literature with real life, directly and unselfconsciously. Art verifies and explains their experiences without their being aware of technique.

We, as teachers, choose a particular novel not just because we think it will be "teachable," but because we like it. It engrosses us sufficiently so that we are willing to read and reread it. The pleasure we feel is an intricate mixture of interest in subject and theme and an appreciation of style, form, and texture; much of our enjoyment is personal and unexamined. Each of us has a range of interest and satisfaction: above it, the reading is too difficult to yield pleasure easily; below it, the subject or its handling is offensive or dull. In choosing to teach a book we like, we may be placing enjoyment beyond the reach of many of our students. Though Thoreau advises standing on tiptoe to read, most of us can endure only a limited number of "improving" books at any one time. For our students, most books are "improving" books, difficult partly because they must be read on schedule. But even with the implicit coercion of class requirements, students usually make some effort to find pleasure in assigned fiction. We need to encourage their enjoyment by selecting books within their range of interest and pleasure.

Interest in the Classics

Choosing literature within the students' range need not mean pandering to fads or doubtful taste, nor need it mean stepping out of our own range. Most of us are not half as aesthetic as we think we are. We like books that satisfy our curiosity as well as books that make us feel well read. Booth (1961) contends that reading satisfies a basic need to learn. This is borne out, I believe, in my students' interest in Greek tragedy and mythology. They think they ought to know fundamental material even when the content is incompatible with their own beliefs and observations. They wish to know something great and classic; for this they have come to college, and for such works they are willing to hold their own values and convictions temporarily in abeyance. They will usually make the same concessions for Shakespeare—and more easily because they often find something romantic or amusing in his plays.

Before I figured out these things about students' interests, I mistook their respect for known classics for an interest in the great themes in literature, and I chose to teach them from Irving Howe's collection of *Seven Short Novels.* I encountered antipathy and boredom. I heard depressing comments about "all that death" and the "dumb characters." Short as the selections were, I was unable to impress my students with the rich variety of masterful styles. After I took them beyond Sophocles and Shakespeare, their reverence for learning paled. They had not come to college to read Henry James or even Tolstoy. The subjects and ideas and characters had to be closer to their own experiences. Considering our society's adoration for youth and terror of age and death, how could I get them to empathize with Tolstoy's Gerasim? Unacquainted as they were with humility, how could these freshmen feel anything for Flaubert's old servant with her stuffed parrot? With their wholesome psyches and ever-adjustable personalities, could they be anything but irritated by James's neurotic pupil and his tutor? Almost nothing in these stories coincided with their limited experiences. Only "The Secret Sharer" touched their imaginations and suspended their disbelief.

My students rejected anguish, despair, and death. Each of us brings to any work of literature our own associations and faculties for understanding. In an essay on taste, Lucas (1957) points out differences in response: "One can *never* rationally say (as people persistently do, with that familiar air of mingled sorrow and superiority), 'But you *ought* to like it.'" Art, in providing form for our perceptions and experiences, also conveys and elicits feeling. Our students are unable to enjoy reading that doesn't involve their emotions. Their limitations may arouse intolerance in some English teachers; we are, nevertheless, paid to expand students' minds. I tried. I worked hard to teach stories I liked, and I probably implied that my students ought to like them. But they did not like the stories; they did not work hard—and they did not learn. My alternative lay in confronting my own limitations. I needed to learn how to engage students' interest in the study of literature.

Sources of Reading Pleasure

Like most English teachers, I have always liked to read; I respond to art with pleasure. This pleasure, according to Arnheim (1966), is "no more specific than the purr of a cat." He also compares pleasure in reading to that in eating, a comparison that does not seem to reflect the variety and complexity of reading experiences (although it does suggest parallels of taste and forced feeding). Reading provides enjoyment and fulfillment of needs on many levels. Good readers can't describe the pleasure, nor explain why it leads to more diverse and more demanding reading. Feelings, perceptions, and understanding all seem to compel readers toward more selectivity and even toward active critical appraisal. But we know our students are not good readers and are seldom ready to join our usual game of examining form and style. If they are to get anything out of reading, they must be ensnared by a subject they can understand and characters for whom they can feel something. To have meaning for readers, fiction must objectify and externalize *their* human conflicts. Emotion provides the energy of art—and the pleasure. However, we want our students to do more than purr.

Reading pleasure derives in part from the distance and pattern the author gives to experience. Despite their empathy, readers can retain their perspective and feel safe in the knowledge that they will see events and characters whole. Readers survive the most perilous adventures and devastating losses. The dangers, demands, and randomness of life seldom permit such satisfaction as fiction provides. Fiction allows us to confront aspects of our lives and images of our natures. Fiction allows but does not insist.

Three Responses to Fiction

My students, however, insist whenever possible on confronting their problems and images. They bring their crises to class. They seek involvement—personal and intense—and if such participation is lacking, they complain rather precisely that they "can't relate to that."

Their behavior exhibits each of the primary responses to fiction delineated by Lesser in *Fiction and the Unconscious* (1957). He says every reader reacts by identifying, analogizing, and appraising. In the last twenty years, Jungian theories and mind/brain research have modified our definitions of "the unconscious," but the substance of Lesser's theories remains. We can understand "unconscious" to encompass the perceptions and feelings not yet willingly or totally accepted by the more rational or logical part of us. Or we can simply term the responses innate, or natural.

Identifying

Of the responses described by Lesser, identifying seems most familiar to us; we have used it as a means of stimulating class discussions. But identification is more than simply putting ourselves in another's place; it expands our capacities for discernment and compassion. We recognize ourselves in several characters simultaneously, the depth and dispersion of identities varying with our self-knowledge. Identification relies on both understanding and imagination. Fiction allows us to see our own complexity—to see ourselves as villains and heroes, as victims and oppressors. Part of our satisfaction lies in recognizing our all-too-human condition—in knowing we are like others, in knowing we are not alone. Those who prefer not to look at their own contradictory natures are allowed to be spectators. Fiction does not insist on conscious identification.

Analogizing

The second response is a creative one, and one we are likely to regard as peripheral to literature. Analogizing is a bit like daydreaming; it may seem totally irrelevant to the teacher who is trying to attend to the text. According to Lesser, however, we all create parallels while we read. Satisfaction may lie in remembering or inventing a pleasant event or in reconstructing and altering a painful one. Some of my students recalled their first love as they read "Araby." The process of analogy does not detract from the reading but reflects and enhances its meaning. Operating like a photomontage, like counterpoint or harmony, analogizing makes few demands on our attention while adding depth to our reading pleasure.

Appraising

Appraising is the third response, and it sounds much like something we ought to be teaching. It only faintly resembles literary criticism, however. Appraising is a basic, continuous effort to comprehend events. We incessantly compare, infer, interpret, categorize; we test fiction against our own experiences. Students from California valley towns, for example, examine Steinbeck's views of migrant workers against their own backgrounds. This innate tendency to evaluate involves numerous aspects of learning. As teachers, we can help students to expand and trust this tendency, and to develop bases and points of reference for their appraisals.

Each of the three responses to fiction arises from content, the most accessible aspect of literature. For the experienced reader, content provides only a small part of the pleasure, but for most of my students, content is a central concern. They are innocent of the effects of style, form, and texture—and will remain so unless they can "relate to" the content. To tell them form cannot be divorced from meaning, to say the characters and settings and situations exist only as the author chooses to present them, is worse than useless. They have heard it before and still do not understand.

The power of content and of the students' need to respond to stories directly, as if there were no writer, showed clearly in my students' reactions to two stories by Saul Bellow. *Seize the Day* is a very short novel with lots of dialogue and little description. It does not even have a difficult vocabulary. Despite these advantages, very few of my students liked the story at all. They are not especially tolerant, and the excesses of Wilkie puzzled and disgusted them. They could not empathize with him: he is a New Yorker and a loser, and they are neither. They could not see why he was hanging around the hotel, sucking up to his father, and drinking Cokes for breakfast. They would have left town, after a healthful instant breakfast, and pumped gas in Fresno rather than flounder like Wilkie.

I have no idea why, when I abandoned the book in which *Seize the Day* was the least popular story, I chose to teach Bellow's *Henderson the Rain King*. The novel is long and full of strange people with even stranger names. It includes long, descriptive passages and flashbacks that elude sequence. Certainly Henderson's behavior is bizarre and his aging person is repulsive by all the standards one would expect my students to apply. But Henderson is a seeker, a believer, a lover of life and action. My students loved him. They evidently shared Wayne Booth's willingness to "subordinate mind and heart to the book" and to enjoy it to the full. Taken by Henderson, they were ready to surrender all resistance and to examine the story in every way—to discuss structure, themes, motifs, and language. Entrée was achieved because of the novel's content and the students' powerfully involved emotions.

As English teachers, our greatest limitation is not in how we teach but in being unaware of what we teach. In literature we emphasize form, style, genre, canon, and critical modes; in composition we expound on thesis, logic, coherence, and commas. We behave as if our own sophisticated enjoyment were derived from an art devoid of feeling and meaning. Any piece of literature seems to serve our purposes: we can remain aloof from content and emotion—from the whole range of human response to humane letters. We can do this. But look where it gets us.

4 Traditional Literature for Nontraditional Students

Susan R. Blau
Middlesex Community College

Like those of Theresa Enroth, Susan Blau's suggestions about teaching literature to first-year college students emphasize the concrete, content-oriented approach. She finds that traditional literature is a proper and rewarding study, but that traditional methods of instruction need rethinking. She begins her discussion with a call for demystification of the reading of literature. Her specific suggestions about the student-centered approach to literature underline the importance of studying the artists, the boundary-expanding nature of creativity, and the students' intense personal involvement with what they read.

Sometimes I get the feeling that the teaching of literature is an anachronism—at least for my students. Are dental hygienists, secretaries, and mechanics going to read or care about McMurphy's battle with Big Nurse or Holden's breakdown or, even more remotely, Ahab's manic search for a whale, when they can have totally absorbing entertainment just by flicking a switch? Haven't we already been ushered, some of us kicking and screaming, into McLuhan's postliterate society?

The case has been made many times, of course, for the power and importance of literature in defining our humanness. There is no need to convince an avid reader of this. Yet how can we show the mental health technicians that McMurphy, Holden, and Ahab can speak to their needs and concerns as individuals as well as paraprofessionals?

If the problem is that literature seems inaccessible to our students, the solution does not lie in bowing to the inevitable onslaught of the McLuhan age and teaching media in place of reading. It's as silly to throw out the literature as it is to throw out the students. The answer is either to find literature that is accessible, as Marsha Oliver suggests in her approach to nontraditional literature for the "new student," or to find a way to bring traditional literature to the nontraditional student.

Demystifying Literature

My approach to teaching literature in the first college years begins with demystification. Many of my students have a sense that reading literature is an elite, intellectual activity that is beyond their reach. I would like to help them see that reading and understanding literature are not arcane rituals practiced only in the presence of the high priests and priestesses of Comp. and Lit. II. We have to destroy the myth that literature is something that one either innately understands or will never comprehend. We go about destroying this myth for our students by destroying it for ourselves—an unnerving thing for English teachers to do.

There are, of course, aspects of literature that our students will never be able to understand. I am not suggesting that all of our knowledge is accessible to them. But I am suggesting that most college people are capable of reading and enjoying literature, and on a fairly sophisticated level, if we allow them to become initiated into literature from a position of pleasure rather than one of painful inaccessibility.

Approaching Literature by Studying Writers

In the preceding essay Theresa Enroth focuses upon the specific content of a literary work. It is, after all, the concrete and not the abstract which attracts our students. Another concrete and enjoyable way to approach literature is through a study of the artist.

Intimidated by the fear of committing the intentional or biographical fallacy, I have taught literature as I was taught it in the waning days of New Criticism, as though books appeared on the literary landscape fully formed and leather bound, unsullied by human hands. Not only does this view separate the artist from the work, but, more seriously, it also prevents the reader from knowing that writing and reading are human activities beset by anxiety and climaxed—sometimes—by triumph.

Literary criticism, whether it is in the formalistic or any of the aesthetic, ethical, or scientific modes, has been the traditional way in which students are introduced to literature. Yet the very act of using formal criticism as a way to understand a book elevates the importance of the critical apparatus and sidesteps the direct reading experience. Eventually criticism becomes larger than the literature it is supposed to examine. As Clark (1976) writes, "No longer simply the hand-maiden of literature, criticism has become more clearly and more clamorously an intellectual enterprise in its own right . . ." (p. 224).

It seems to me that many of the traditional approaches to critical exposition not only overpower but also limit the literature. They limit because they suggest that the literature (and therefore the human experience it expresses) can be looked at in one way, divorced from any larger social, political, moral, historical, or artistic reality. Such specialization may be fine for scholars and perhaps even for upper-division students; but my students have too much fragmentation in their lives already. They are plugged into Psych. at ten, Soc. at eleven, and Lit. at twelve as if there were no common ground among them. Even the abbreviated titles alienate. Students are delighted, and surprised, when a bit of knowledge from Psych. can be applied in Lit.

To me a more interesting approach would be to use the life and times of the person behind the words to show the historical, political, social, and ethical worlds in which the artist lived and worked. Explore how these worldly conditions, as well as the circumstances of the artist's life, influenced his or her world view. Show the artist in context with the world, the times, and the artistic environment. Out of this grounding in the artist's personal landscape the work of art grows and takes on new meaning.

In an introductory literature course, seventeenth- or eighteenth-century poets often are rejected in favor of modern poets, who, we are told, can "speak" to the students. Students are already familiar with at least some of the nuances of the world and time in which the modern poets write. But students also can relate to poets from other times and other places and gain access to areas of knowledge formerly closed to them.

Take an extreme example: Puritan American poetry is taught, if at all, in the upper-division courses. Yet an incredible richness of experience is lost by this omission in the first college years. So much of our modern society—our literature, myths, and ethics—is rooted in the Puritan era. Living in a seventeenth-century theocracy was substantially different from living in a twentieth-century democracy, and yet the closeness of our modern society to Puritan New England is undeniable. Not only have we inherited the Puritan work ethic, but we also can trace many of our national attitudes toward sex, religion, and politics to our colonial ancestors.

There is no reason not to teach traditional colonial literature to first-year students. One could introduce them to Anne Bradstreet, a woman who lived on the edge of the American frontier (at that time Ipswich, Massachusetts), often separated from her husband. While raising eight children, she still managed to find time to write some impressive, very personal poetry. A study of Bradstreet's poetry would tie in with topics such as Puritanism, the role of women, and the place of poetry in Puritan life. Considering the conditions of the period, the fact that Anne Bradstreet wrote poetry at all becomes an extraordinary act, a quiet kind of rebellion, and the poems she wrote can be approached with a sense of their context. They no longer seem pulled out of time and place, but part of a world that is comprehensible today. Modern students, without knowledge of the woman and her times, might understand the wit but miss the courage in this poetic retort to her critics:

> I am obnoxious to each carping tongue
> Who says my hand a needle better fits,
> A poet's pen all scorn I should thus wrong,
> For such despite they cast on female wits:
> If what I do prove well, it won't advance,
> They'll say it's stolen, or else it was by chance.

I suggest that Anne Bradstreet can indeed speak to our students.

Understanding the writer in context with the time provides the student with a way into the literature. Yet the writer must not overwhelm the work of art, and so it is important to make the leap from the person to the persona, from the real person to the fictional world. Without this, there is danger that some students may dismiss Sylvia Plath's poetry because suicide is immoral, or ignore "Howl" because they don't like homosexuals. Or, to the other extreme, they may become so fascinated by Emily Dickinson's person that they neglect her persona.

Approaching Literature by Studying Creativity

What I have been concerned with up to this point is the use of the artist's role in the creative process as an entrance to the literary work. The next aspect I would like to examine is the artistic process itself. What is it? What is it that we do when we write or paint or build or compose? The complexity of the question makes it almost unapproachable. However, a few years ago I had an insight into the nature of creativity, which relates in part to teaching literature.

After our family Thanksgiving dinner in Washington, D. C., I wandered off for a few hours to a van Gogh exhibit at the Phillips

Gallery. After viewing two rooms of van Gogh pictures, one particular self-portrait, which I had seen many times in reproductions, ensnared me. I'm not sure whether it was the wine-laced meal or the intensity of my immersion in van Gogh, but it suddenly seemed clear to me that the boldness and the anger of the brush strokes in the portrait were not my world translated through an artist's eyes, but a world I'd never seen and probably never would. It seemed to me then, and still does, that the artist sees another dimension of reality, or, in fact, creates a personal reality that is substantially different from mine. I think of Yeats, Eliot, Faulkner, Joyce, C. S. Lewis.

If this theory is true, then it becomes easier to see the task of the literature teacher as one of "expanding horizons"—a trite metaphor perhaps, but also a powerful one if the horizons are the outer limits of our defined world. I don't suggest that this is a mystical or inspired experience, although it may indeed be. After all, van Gogh's paintings are often described as extraordinary or works of genius. Certainly the artistic expression of his reality has touched many and perhaps has even caused some to shift their focus on the world. However, this experience may also be the down-to-earth realization that the heroes of the world are not necessarily white, middle-class, or male. This realization, too, changes forever the way one views life. The student has to learn to push away the limitations of the known world, just as in the parlor-game test for creativity the participant can connect the nine dots with four continuous straight lines only by going beyond the visually suggested boundaries (see Figure 1).

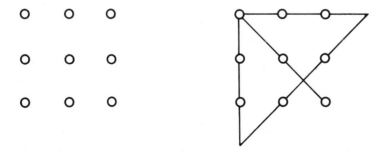

Fig. 1. Enlarging one's vision: a test of perception.

This view of creativity as the expansion of traditional boundaries, along with the artist-centered approach to literature, suggests
a connection between literature and composition. It also suggests a
reordering of the traditional sequence of composition first, then
literature. If we begin with the artist and the artist's world, the
student will see by example how a real person exists, experiences a
certain set of circumstances, and then translates this into art. Writing then moves away from "themewriting," which William E. Coles,
Jr. (1971) describes as "no more than a kind of transcription, a
known, not a way of knowing, a way of saying something, not
something being said." Writing becomes the creative act of expressing a subjective reality. It becomes art.

When we examine literature as a personal statement about an
artist's perception of the world, emphasizing that it is an expression of something important that the artist needs to say, it quickly
becomes a concrete example of what we want our students to do
when they write. As van Gogh translated his sense of the world
onto canvas, inexperienced writers also must study their worlds,
outer and inner, and from this examination find something important to say. In this way literature can serve not only as an example
of how and why to write but also, by opening their world to other
places and other people, may give the students something more to
say. It makes sense, therefore, to begin a freshman English course
with a study of literature and then move to writing.

Approaching Literature through Personal Involvement

My final suggestion about making literature accessible to students
is perhaps the most logical. When an artist has a personal vision
that is translated into a work of art, this private perception of life
is brought into the public world. Once "The Love Song of J. Alfred
Prufrock" was published, Eliot's vision of modern man was no
longer his alone but in the public domain. However, a reader can
bring this public statement back to the private, subjective world.
The reader of "Prufrock" in a sense re-creates the work by filter-
ing Eliot's images, words, and rhythms through personal experiences and biases. The eighteen-year-old student reacts to Prufrock's
lament "I grow old" with less sympathy, but perhaps more objectivity, than the middle-aged reader. The completion of the movement from writer to reader allows literature to be a powerful,
intensely personal experience. And so the highly subjective approach to literature seems not only logical but appropriate.

I want to lead my students to the point where they can use

literature to learn about themselves and the larger world. Kafka remarked that "a book should serve as the axe for the frozen sea within us." That same axe can be used to chip away at the perceptual rime which limits our view of the external world.

Teachers of the very personal, very subjective approach to literature have often been called self-serving and nonacademic. I have repeated to my students the enjoinder to be objective, to look at Big Nurse as a symbol rather than as a person—hoping all the while that they will come to be deeply offended by the oppression of the human spirit which she symbolizes *for me*. I come to literature because it touches me, speaks to me. My students may never have this experience if I deny them the power of their personal involvement by demanding objectivity, expecting the humanistic values expressed in literature to somehow rub off.

In this personal, subjective approach, literature can be liberating in an idealistic, humanistic sense as well as in a pragmatic, political sense. It can be an escape from the narrowness of the places in which we all dwell.

On the personal level, I want my students, through their involvement with literature, to begin to understand tolerance, to concede that other people may have perceptions of reality and live in worlds that are different from their own, but which are still okay. I want them to understand that they are not alone but still unique by seeing the commonness of human problems and the variety of responses to these problems. I want them to understand that not all problems can be solved.

Using Literature to Interpret Social Values

In a political sense, I want to help my students extricate themselves from the self-limiting definitions of their class-oriented lives and values, and begin to be aware of a world bigger than they thought—and with more options. It is a common experience while teaching "The Unknown Citizen" to realize that many students so completely accept the values which W. H. Auden is satirizing that they initially fail to detect the irony. The poem then becomes a fine tool for exploring commonly accepted assumptions about material possessions, technology, conformity, and individuality. The woods are full of writers who can shock readers out of their complacency and perhaps help them move from what things are to what they might be.

It seems to me that this is one of the most radical things that can be done in any education system, to help students break away from the self- and culturally-limiting definitions and to touch their world with a compassionate and realistic sense of what can be changed. This is especially radical if we are dismayed at education today as it creates individuals who fit comfortably into our fast-moving, progress-oriented, scientifically based technocracy—individuals who don't question, write poems, or make revolutions. I see literature as the perfect vehicle to reawaken students to a sense of their shared humanity. Literature is of human creation and as such reflects the human condition in its squalor and in its beauty.

If literature is to continue to be presented as an area of important human concern, then teachers of literature will have to shake themselves loose from the traditional assumptions about how it should be taught. My suggestions about the need to demystify literature, the role of the artist, the creative process, and the subjective mode are offered not as a solution, but to provoke thought about the teaching of literature to the students who are in our classrooms now. It is these students who must be touched by literature, who must find in literature the humanizing forces that we claim are there.

5 Popular Fiction: Remedial Literature for New Students

Marsha M. Oliver
Anoka-Ramsey Community College

Many writers in this collection argue that exposure to humanities courses is vital for *all* students. Marsha Oliver makes the practical observation that new students won't awaken to the humanizing possibilities of literature if they refuse to enroll in literature courses. In her experience, weak readers *will* sign up for an elective class in popular fiction. Such a course gives them the chance to read material that traditional students read before coming to college and to raise their level of reading maturity so they can appreciate and understand serious literature.

Many two-year colleges have shifted their original mission: where formerly they prepared students for transfer to four-year institutions, they now offer them a marketable skill. Often these colleges began with traditional liberal arts requirements, but pressure from government funding agencies, state universities, and community members forced them to limit their transfer courses and expand their two-year vocational programs. This situation occurs primarily in open-door colleges serving low-income communities. Because economic survival is the most immediate concern of students at these schools, they are reluctant to enroll in courses which they regard as superfluous—courses for which they must pay tuition but which are not directly related to future jobs.

Instructors in the vocational programs often support the students by lobbying for fewer humanities requirements, not wanting students to "waste" their limited time and money on courses that have no immediate practical return. The administration usually accedes to the demands of the vocational lobbyists, rationalizing that those who are really interested in humanities classes will select them as electives. But this is often not the case, particularly with traditional literature courses; in colleges where literature is no longer required for graduation, classes are often disappointingly small. Because of past experiences with the "highbrow" tastes of English instructors, students decide not to enroll in elective courses that deal with serious fiction and poetry. They have sampled the selected readings in the required freshman composition course and have found them too abstract for their interest and reading level. In one midwestern college, for example, the instructors chose to teach Melville's *Billy Budd* in their composition classes during the Vietnam protest years, thinking students would find the conflict between institutional authority and personal conscience "relevant." Only the teachers were aroused; the students fell asleep, complaining that the story was boring, difficult, and depressing. As soon as the literature requirement was waived they abandoned this necessary exposure to the humanities for more practical, "real world" courses. Many left school with two-year degree certificates but no courses in literature, history, or philosophy.

In an attempt to attract more students into literature classes, some instructors have rearranged the material, hoping that perhaps a thematic approach would be more appealing than the traditional historical grouping. What they failed to realize is that no matter how attractively serious or mainstream literature is packaged—as "Love Themes in Fiction," or "Tortured Heroes in Drama and Poetry," for instance—it still requires a level of reading maturity that many students have not achieved, particularly those called "new students" by Cross (1971). She describes them as people who have never been successful in school, who feel intimidated in the classroom, and who are suspicious of information that challenges their values. Few have ever read for pleasure, and most were raised in environments where reading was not emphasized. Truly members of the McLuhan generation, they spent their formative years in front of the television set; now that they are in college, they often cut noon classes to watch soap operas on the TV in the student lounge.

Students entering private four-year colleges, in contrast, have had more reading experience than their new-student peers, although admittedly they read less than their pretelevision parents. They enroll in college literature classes, ready at least to *begin* looking at mainstream fiction because they have experienced the normal stages of reading development, common to most educated people, during childhood and adolescence. In the early grades they read series books about daring young detectives, athletes, or orphans and then moved to popular or category fiction, with older heroes and heroines, during junior high or high school, while at the same time starting on some of the classics. By college their reading skill has reached the point where they are comfortable with literary devices such as allusions, flashbacks, or digressions—all puzzling to the new students in the two-year colleges who lack this background. The ability to appreciate and understand serious literature seems to come *after* a person has had a wide exposure to action-filled plots, strong heroes and heroines, and the other characteristics of popular fiction.

Popular Fiction as a Literary Option

Operating from this premise, some two-year college English instructors have considered offering courses in popular fiction to supply the new students with this missing stage of adolescent reading development. But when they suggest revising their curriculum to include courses whose material follows a predetermined formula—such as westerns, mysteries, or adventure stories—their traditionally educated colleagues and administrators often demur, despite assurances that first-rate popular works will be studied—not books by Mickey Spillane or Barbara Cartland. They feel that popular fiction should not be taught at the college level because it is not intellectually demanding and is lacking in literary merit. Common arguments parallel those of Perrine (1959), who states in the introduction to *Story and Structure* that popular fiction is not an appropriate topic for college study because it offers the reader pleasure rather than a "keener awareness of what it is to be a human being." He criticizes the sympathetic, action-filled plots, the reliance on suspense and gimmicks, and the fact that popular fiction slips "smoothly through the mind, requiring little mental effort." Worst of all, it gives the reader "superficial attitudes toward life" and "false concepts and false expectations of reality."

These comments should not deter English instructors from teaching popular fiction to the new students, for two reasons. First, Perrine's arguments apply to students who presumably have passed through the adolescent stage of literature appreciation; for them, such a course would not be particularly challenging or worthwhile. The new students, on the other hand, didn't learn of Nancy Drew or the Hardy boys until they saw them on television. Finishing a two-hundred-page mystery novel *is* a demanding task for those with eighth-grade reading skills. Second, good popular fiction is not the pap that Perrine makes it out to be, although it is written for a different purpose than serious literature. A popular writer tries to provide readers with a pleasurable escape from reality, while a serious writer tries to give insight into reality. The best examples of both kinds of fiction usually achieve both goals, differing only in degree of subtlety. The literary merit of a popular story or novel depends on how imaginatively the writer works within the boundaries of certain conventions rather than on how creatively he or she explores new territory. The best popular writers transform stock characters, trite plots, and implausible situations into something new and entertaining. Such writers vary old stereotypes, invent ingenious twists to familiar plots, and create such a rich fantasy world that the reader's interest is sustained for long periods of time. Serious writers work with the same basic material but they are not limited by the demands of a formulaic convention.

Stereotyped Characters

Stereotypical characters are an essential part of popular writing, usually being too good or too bad to resemble real people; in contrast, serious writers try to present characters who behave the way humans really act in specific situations. Cawelti (1976) explains that good popular writers vitalize the old stereotypes, "often adding new elements, by showing us some new and unexpected facet, or by relating them to other stereotypes in a particularly expressive fashion." One means of achieving this vitalization is to invent contradictory traits for what otherwise appears to be a stereotyped character. For example, Sherlock Holmes, although a direct imitation of Poe's C. Auguste Dupin, has such a unique personality that readers have been fascinated by him for decades. Holmes is a master of rational analysis, but he smokes opium, and once, in a burst of patriotic passion, he uses his pistol to shoot the queen's initials in the wall.

   An author also can give significant touches of human complexity or frailty to a stereotyped figure, as Georges Simenon does with Inspector Maigret. In the course of one investigation, Maigret feels attracted to a forty-one-year-old alcoholic murderess. As he tries to understand his conflicting emotions, the reader gains at least something of a "keener awareness of what it is to be a human being," despite the fact that Maigret is cut from the same bolt as Dupin and Holmes.

Predictable Plot and Setting

It is true that plots in popular fiction are predictable; in contrast, choices made by the characters determine the plots of serious literature, regardless of whether these choices disappoint the readers' wishes for a resolution or a happy ending. A popular work is written according to a formula that readers have found pleasing over the years, and its success cannot be judged by the originality of its plot. The best popular writing teases its readers by threatening to break the formulaic pattern and then reassures them by returning to a familiar structure. The charm of formulaic literature comes from the repetition of a formula, but in a different way, that makes the reader's expected experience more intense—without fundamentally altering it.

Popular writers don't try to heighten their readers' awareness of reality as do the writers of serious fiction. The best popular authors present a slightly remote, ideal world which the audience can still accept as having some connection with reality—similar to the "primary world" invented by authors of fantasies. The formula story creates its own field of reference which relates to the readers' previous familiarity with the formula itself instead of to their actual experience with life. The result is to make them less inclined to measure the story in terms of their ordinary standards of plausibility. If writers establish a successful imaginary world, they can stretch the limits of plausibility and still retain eager reader acceptance. At the end of John Buchan's *The Thirty-Nine Steps*, the readers are so enmeshed in his primary world that they barely notice how unlikely is the discovery of the mysterious steps. Works like the Sherlock Holmes stories or *Gone with the Wind* do contain stereotypical characters, unlikely situations, and obsolete themes and values; but they give readers pleasure, years after they were written, because their fantasy world is so complete and interesting.

The literary merit of popular fiction, then, depends on how imaginatively writers combine familiar ingredients to take the reader away from the real world, not on how creatively they invent unusual characters and situations to take the reader more deeply into reality. Although some may consider popular fiction as frivolous, good popular writing is composed of the same basic elements as mainstream literature, making it appropriate for introducing weak readers to elementary literary concepts and principles.

Benefits of Popular Fiction

Half of the students at the college where I teach are reading at the eighth-grade level or below, and almost all of them would be called new students by Cross. We have successfully taught courses in popular fiction to these students and we find that they can understand concepts such as conflict, character, plot, suspense, point of view, and style when they discuss them in relation to a book they can actually read. They soon realize how much more satisfying a complex character is than a flat one when they compare the characters in Agatha Christie's *Murder on the Orient Express* with those in Dorothy Sayers's *Gaudy Night*.

In addition to giving the new students a foundation on which they can eventually build an appreciation of serious literature, a course in popular fiction answers many of their personal needs. Vocationally oriented people who have previously met with little academic success usually hesitate to sign up for one of these classes; but if we assure them that they will be able to do the work, and tempt them with tidbits from the assigned readings (corpses stuffed up chimneys, and so on), they agree to try it for a few days. Once in the classroom, they are surprised that they can read the books and comment on them intelligently. Their confidence increases as they discover that they do have some critical judgment and that they can distinguish between hack work and good writing. When they read that Lord Peter Wimsey (in *Murder Must Advertise*) dives from the top of a high fountain into a shallow pool and emerges unscathed, they are able to discuss the limits of plausibility. They have no problem in understanding the importance of setting and its relation to suspense when they read about Grimpen Mire in *The Hound of the Baskervilles*. They notice the sentimentality in gothic romances. As their confidence grows, their hostility toward "impractical" intellectual activities decreases.

Reading and discussing popular fiction also sharpens their ability to think critically; as students identify the conventional and simplistic values often present in popular writing, they learn to recognize and evaluate their own assumptions. For example, many books provide opportunities for discussing sex role stereotypes. Students can analyze masculinity as presented in hard-boiled detective novels and then decide whether a "real man" actually is a hard-drinking, hard-fighting, emotionally uninvolved loner. Gothic romances present an excellent chance to discuss a woman's role in society. The gothic convention demands that the heroine be a poor, passive, friendless girl who fears she isn't pretty (but she is). She has few redeeming features, being ordinary, poorly educated, and characterless—but she is good with children. Some of our mature women students identified with this passive heroine at the start of one mystery course, having read endless variations of the gothic formula in their spare time. But after discussing a gothic romance in class, they realized how they differed from this character, particularly since they had made the independent decision to attend college and perhaps prepare for a career.

Some students are able to make the leap to serious fiction after they understand how it differs from popular writing, if they don't feel threatened by aesthetic values different from their own. At my school, traditional classes in poetry, short story, and American literature averaged about six students each during one spring term several years ago. After we began offering courses in popular fiction, enrollment in these classes increased, and in spring 1977 each of these subjects drew about twenty-five students. Roughly one-third of those in the so-called traditional courses had previously taken a class in popular fiction. People who formerly would never have chosen even one literature elective are now taking two.

These results suggest that it is unrealistic to expect pragmatic students with weak reading skills to choose a course that examines the works of James, Conrad, or Melville. We should take into account their level of reading maturity by providing them with the chance to experience the adolescent stage of literary appreciation. We aren't serving the needs of all our students if we limit our literature offerings to traditional courses that attract only a few people each term. Even if these new students have enrolled in college primarily to improve their chances in the job market, we should entice them into courses that expose them to a more creative and humanizing alternative for their leisure hours than watching television. Popular fiction, possessing its own kind of literary merit, is one way to introduce inexperienced readers to the pleasures of escape fiction. Some will gain the confidence and conceptual understanding necessary to advance to mainstream literature and the adult level of reading maturity.

6 Characteristics of Contemporary Native American Literature

Craig Lesley
Clackamas Community College

Craig Lesley's essay reflects Susan Blau's idea that one effective approach to literature includes a study of the writer and the world in which he or she lives. This approach is particularly pertinent to the study of Native American literature. The perceptions and values of Native Americans differ from those of Anglos because of the many differences between the two cultures. Therefore, a proper investigation of Native American literature necessarily includes some understanding of the Native American's world view. Lesley also suggests that the process of studying Native American literature and culture will enable Anglos to gain another perspective from which to evaluate their own ideas of the way things are.

When N. Scott Momaday was awarded the Pulitzer Prize in 1969 for *House Made of Dawn*, contemporary Native American literature gained national recognition. The excellent Indian anthologies and novels published since Momaday's work demonstrate that Native American literature continues to be a major literary force. Nonetheless, many readers remain puzzled about the new Indian writers because their works cannot be explicated fully according to familiar literary criteria.

This bewilderment decreases if readers bear in mind that the Indian writer's perceptions, values, and culture are different from those familiar to the Anglo. Once these differences are accounted for, we can better understand contemporary Indian writing.

By studying Native American literature we learn that there are other ways of perceiving, other values operating; in the process, we increase our understanding of the Native American's perceptions and values. We also gain another perspective from which to view our own idea of the way things are.

Importance of the Land

An investigation of contemporary Native American writing reveals
the close relationship between the writer's work and the land. Native Americans understand themselves in relation to the landscape.
There is reciprocity between the Native American and the land, a
participation of the Indian in the landscape. This strong connection is readily apparent in most works by contemporary Native
American authors. Momaday explains, "Man understands himself
in relation to the tree over here and the mountain over here and
the river and naturally operates out of that environment, operates
immediately out of it.... Man understands that he is obligated
in certain ways to the landscape, that he is responsible for it, that
he shares in the spirit of place" ("A Conversation with N. Scott
Momaday," 1976, p. 19).

Leslie Silko, a Laguna Pueblo writer, demonstrates an understanding of Momaday's concept as she explains, "I grew up at Laguna Pueblo. . . . This place that I am from is everything I am as a
writer and human being." She understands also Momaday's discussion of man's relation to a tree or a mountain. In the introduction
to her book *Laguna Woman* (1974), Silko describes her great-
grandmother's place at Laguna and the large cottonwood tree
there. In her short story "The Man to Send Rain Clouds," Silko
uses the cottonwood as a focal point: "They found him under a
big cottonwood tree. His Levi jacket and pants were faded a light-
blue so that he had been easy to find. The big cottonwood tree
stood apart from a small grove of winterbare cottonwoods which
grew in the wide, sandy arroyo" (Rosen, 1974, p. 3).

Search for the Center

This close relationship to the land enables Native Americans to
have a sense of a "center," a place where they belong. Frequently,
the center is pictured as a hoop. In "The Great Vision" chapter of
Black Elk Speaks (Neihardt, 1961), the Oglala Sioux holy man reveals the significance of the center when he recalls the Voice which
told him in his youth, "Behold the circle of the nation's hoop, for
it is holy, being endless, and thus all powers shall be one power in
the people without end" (p. 35). At the conclusion of his work,
after assessing the slaughter at Wounded Knee, Black Elk states,
"And I, to whom so great a vision was given in my youth,—you see
me now a pitiful old man who has done nothing, for the nation's

hoop is broken and scattered. There is no center any longer, and the sacred tree is dead" (p. 276).

In spite of Black Elk's disillusionment, the idea of the center remains an integral part of Native American perception and a major characteristic of their literature. If, as many have noted, the theme of twentieth-century literature is the search for the self and the country of the self, the Native American's search ends at the center. Much of contemporary Indian literature attempts to express the reality of the center and to encourage discovery of the center.

Silko's novel *Ceremony* (1977) traces the attempts of Tayo, an Indian World War II veteran, to regain health and mental equilibrium after his discharge and return to the Southwest. A contemporary medicine man finally counteracts the illness with a ceremony designed to return Tayo's awareness of the center. The main image of this ceremony is the hoop. The medicine man chants (p. 143):

> I will bring you through my hoop,
> I will bring you back.
> . . . .
> Come home, happily
> Return belonging to your home
> Return to long life and happiness again. . . .

After the ceremony has been performed, Tayo regains his health, his awareness of the center, and his relationship to his land: "The magnetism of the center spread over him smoothly like rainwater down his neck and shoulders; the vacant cool sensation glided over the pain like feather-down wings. It was pulling him back, close to the earth, where the core was cool and silent as mountain stone, . . ." (p. 201).

Momaday's *House Made of Dawn* (1968) also includes a passage that expresses the importance of the center and its relation to the land. His speaker, Abel, remembers: "And that night your grandfather . . . told you stories in the firelight. And you were little and right there in the center of everything, the sacred mountains, the snow-covered mountains and the hills, the gullies and the flats, the sundown and the night, everything—where you were little, where you were and had to be" (p. 157).

Abel's closeness to the center depends on his ties with the land. That closeness is enhanced by the presence of his grandfather. Relatives, clan members, adopted families, tribal elders, and medicine men all give the individual a sense of place in the tribal system, but the influence of the grandparents or great-grandparents is frequently the most important. Silko's close relationship with her great-grandmother indicates this importance: "My mother had to work, so I spent most of my time with my great-grandma, following her around her yard while she watered the holly-hocks and blue morning glories. When I got older I carried the coal bucket inside for her. Her name was Maria Anaya and she was born in Paguate village, north of Old Laguna. . . . She took care of me and my sisters and she told us about how things were when she was a little girl" (Silko, 1974, pp. 34–35).

Relationship to the Past

The closeness of Native Americans to their grandparents, great-grandparents, or great-great-grandparents suggests another part of the Indian's perception that makes the center approachable. The Indian writer works out of a concept of time that is cyclical rather than linear. This involves a concentric continuity whereby the speaker becomes closer to the future (and the past) rather than further removed. Momaday ("A Conversation with N. Scott Momaday," 1976) expresses the Indian's relation to heritage and time as follows:

> I think the storyteller in Indian tradition understands that he is dealing in something that is timeless. He has a sense of its projection into the past. And it's an unlimited kind of projection. I am speaking, I am telling a story, I am doing something that my father's father's father's father's father's father did. That kind of understanding of the past and of a continuity in the human voice is a real element in the oral tradition. And it goes forward in the same way. I am here and what I am doing is back here and it will be here. (p. 21)

In *House Made of Dawn*, Momaday uses three distinct narrative voices to emphasize a sense of continuity and closeness with the past. A mythical voice describes the rituals and the Native American's relation to the land. A historical voice records the life of Abel's grandfather. A contemporary voice indicates the protagonist's (Abel's) perceptions. By interweaving the three voices, Momaday demonstrates the integral dynamic relationships between Abel and his heritage and tribal history.

Because Native American writers understand that they are a part of the past and the past is part of them, they may merge their voices with voices from the past. One example occurs when Charles Ballard, a contemporary Quapaw-Cherokee, takes on the voice of

White Antelope in his poem "Sand Creek." White Antelope, a Cheyenne chief who was slaughtered in the Sand Creek massacre, reportedly folded his arms and sang his death chant "Nothing lives long/Only the earth and the mountain" until he was shot down by the advancing cavalry. Ballard (Rosen, 1975, p. 123) integrates that chant with his poem as his voice and the voice of a historical figure become one:

> And on this day too old to run am I
> Too old for the land of the young
>
> Black Kettle raises the flag
> The air is crisp and cold
> Here at my home I sing
> Nothing lives long
> But the earth and the mountain
>
> White Antelope is my name

The Indian culture is based on the land, the tribe, and the past. Each contributes to the Native American's sense of self and close relation to the center. Contemporary Indian writers' awareness of the center and their belief in their culture save them from the estrangement and bewilderment that permeate the works of their Anglo counterparts—what Theodore Roszak terms "the dispiriting conviction of cosmic absurdity." While Anglo writers find themselves in conflict with their disintegrating culture, where technology and shifting values constantly erode the sense of self, Native American writers embrace their culture and strengthen the self in the process.

Bitterness toward White Culture

Although contemporary Native American literature lacks a voice that expresses alienation toward Indian culture, it contains many voices that express an alienation toward the white culture, "the world of stalking white men" according to the unnamed speaker of Welch's *Winter in the Blood*. The bitterness, hostility, and estrangement of many Native American voices indicate that Indians feel a morally and spiritually inferior culture has encroached upon their own.

Anita Probst's poem "Manifest Destiny" (Niatum, 1975, p. 163) expresses her anger for the intruding white culture:

My mother used to say, Brown Child
of the red sand, wash your feet
with river flowers, climb high
upon the rocks and smile out
the stars. Now as a woman,
I remember a man who said
all Indians are rich
they just don't know how to save,
except by cans of beer.
And like the buffalo, you took my brown
skin and hung it on the wall.
I am gentle, but angry:
Is this how you white men
mount your trophies. Tomorrow, I see
my son; in his eyes there is more than quiet pain—
now blood-red flames bloom anger
and he has yet to live.

The images of "red sand" and "river flowers" and the actions of climbing the rocks and smiling at the stars establish the speaker's close relationship to the natural world. The man who says that Indians don't know how to save and the allusion to buffalo slaughter suggest the white man's lack of sensitivity toward and exploitation of the natural world. A more personal exploitation, probably a sexual one, can be inferred from the brown skin hanging on the wall and the reference to white men mounting trophies. Although brief, the poem effectively expresses a principal conflict between two cultures. The Indian respects and lives in harmony with nature. The white man conquers and exploits nature; in addition, he exploits the Indian—in both general and specific situations.

One method of exploitation involved introducing Indians to alcohol, then acquiring their goods. The current effects of Indian alcohol abuse are all too evident. The poem "Eclipse" (Niatum, 1975, p. 178) exemplifies Probst's general bitterness toward the white man's drink. In addition, it illustrates a personal loss of love through the effects of alcohol:

Black Wolf, naked night-hunter,
you crouch in the corner and growl.
Your howling eclipses my pleas
and the broken bottles rip open your mouth
with the quick surge of an eagle's anger.

You dark man, trying to hide the blood
and spitting it at me in rage;
baring your raw lips and black tongue,
on all fours you crawl from my lodge
and try to find the moon.
Once you said it was in my eyes.

Through the effects of alcohol, the once sensitive lover has become a snarling, crawling beast. James Welch's poem "D-Y Bar" (Niatum, 1975, p. 250) contains similar imagery of man degraded into animal:

> In stunted light, Bear Child tells a story
> to the mirror. He acts his name out,
> creeks muscling gorges fill his glass
> with gumbo. The bear crawls on all fours
> and barks like a dog. Slithering snake-wise
> he balances a nickel on his nose.

The Native American writer understands that, too frequently, overuse of alcohol results in death. The unnamed speaker of Welch's *Winter in the Blood* (1974) lives with the nightmare memory of his father freezing to death after getting drunk in a white man's bar and driving off the road. Although the speaker frequents bars as his father did, eventually he rejects their corrosive influence: "I had had enough of Havre, enough of town, of walking home, hung over, beaten up, or both. I had had enough of the people, the bartenders, the bars . . . ."

The titles of A. K. Redwing's poems are sufficient to express his alienation from and contempt for the white culture. Some examples include "Chrome Babies Eating Chocolate Snowmen," "Two Hookers," "Written in Unbridled Repugnance Near Sioux Falls, Alabama—April 30, 1974," and "A Lost Mohican Visits Hell's Kitchen."

A Vietnam veteran, Redwing frequently points an accusatory finger at the white political-military establishments (Rosen, 1975):

> Clarence Shortbull died.
> >the bullet was aimed decades ago
> by a finger from Washington (p. 134)

and another example:

> A group of touring politicians is shown an elaborate
> >Ball of Chicanery—
> "Brilliant," said the Bozo from Wazoo . . .
> "A commendable piece of artistry," said another.
> >they continue on their tour
> of freshly polished commodes . . .
> playing their role of blind men at a silent movie
>
> An August eagle floats majestically across the sky,
> >He is met by a SAM II . . .
> the feathers land selectively in living rooms
> >from Maine to Seattle . . . (pp. 135-136)

In deploring racism, Redwing concludes:

> Bronze statues of ancient rapists
> applaud tactical squads crunching skulls
> As in the dim light of humanity,
> Adam weeps. . . . (pp. 137–138)

Belief in the Power of Words

Although alienated and angered by the white culture, Probst, Welch, Redwing, and other contemporary Indian writers are not content to express criticism of the way things are. Their words are intended to bring about a change, to improve the way things are. In commenting about her work *Ceremony* (1977), Silko indicates the force behind Indian writing: "This novel is essentially about the powers inherent in the process of storytelling. . . . I feel the power that the stories still have to bring us together, especially when there is loss and grief." Silko's novel (1977, p. 2) includes a poem, also entitled "Ceremony," which further emphasizes the power of the story:

> I will tell you something about stories,
> [he said]
> They aren't just entertainment.
> Don't be fooled.
> They are all we have, you see,
> all we have to fight off
> illness and death.
>
> You don't have anything
> if you don't have the stories.

For the Indian, the word is powerful and sacred. It is powerful enough to change reality. In the introduction to *American Indian Prose and Poetry*, Margot Astrov explains that the word is "the directing agency that stands powerfully behind every 'doing,'" "the reality above all tangible reality" (p. 15). B. L. Whorf's studies among the Hopis indicate that these people believe thought can "determine and direct reality." The corn plant serves to illustrate: "By concentrating his thoughts on the corn plant, [the Hopi] feels he can influence its growth and maturation" (Astrov, 1972, p. 20). In a similar fashion, Crazy Horse dreamed and sang himself into what he felt was another state of consciousness, into another reality. Today, the Indian writer intends to direct his words to effect a change.

Because the word is so powerful for Native Americans, they feel a strong responsibility to use it properly. An ancient song of the Navajo priests reveals the priests' belief in a self within the self, a kind of conscience that ensures the proper use of language (Astrov, 1972, p. 15):

> That standing within me
> Which speaks with me
> Some of these things are always looking at me.
> I am never out of sight.
> Therefore I must tell the truth.
> I hold my word tight to my breast.

This song emphasizes the moral relationship which the Indian feels exists between humans and language. Momaday refers to this relationship in "A Conversation with N. Scott Momaday" (1976). He maintains that "magic, and the idea of magic, is very highly developed . . . It is everywhere. . . . [The Native American writer] is aware of its power. He understands that by exerting the force of language on the physical world, he can bring about actual change. And that's a marvelous attitude. It insures that people use language responsibly" (p. 20).

Henry Realbird, a Crow from Montana, adds another dimension. According to him, serious language among the Crows is referred to as "real talk." Much of real talk reveals the wisdom of the Great Spirit, and may come to humans from other humans, dreams, ghosts, or animals. Real talk is intended to lead or instruct men, and it is never false. If humans hear real talk and ignore it, they may suffer the consequences since it was intended for their instruction. The leaders in the village—the respected elders, chiefs, and medicine men—are ones who understand and listen to real talk.

Because Indians know the power of words and because they feel an obligation to use language responsibly, one can infer that Native American writers would not use language to lie, betray, trick, or cover up. Momaday suggests that the Indian writer is basically honest when he explains, "You know we have a stereotype of the Indian who speaks the truth, the white man who speaks with the forked tongue. . . . There is a basis to the assumption that in an oral culture one deals in the truth. One has a higher regard for language; one tends to take it more seriously. One tends to have a better understanding of what can happen to him if he uses it carelessly, if he abuses it" ("A Conversation with N. Scott Momaday," 1976, p. 21).

The Indian writer's closeness to nature and sensitivity for responsible use of language result in the use of metaphors derived from natural objects, from observations of natural phenomena. Indian names frequently suggest this closeness and responsibility. For example, Henry Realbird's relatives were purposefully named, as he explains in a composition he wrote for a college class:

> My mother's name, Cow-Necklace, was given to her by a clan uncle, Bird Horse. Working as a cowboy, Bird Horse observed that cows with bells around their necks were more trustworthy and dependable than the rest of the lot. By giving my mother the name, he was wishing she too would be a nice and trustworthy person.
>
> My father has two names. His first name, Horse-Catching-Up, is his childhood name. This is a name given to him by his great-grandfather, Medicine Crow. Medicine Crow had a dream in which an old mare was talking to her colt and said, "Horse-Catching-Up." The name means that there are colts every year to the extent that they are all close together age-wise. This denotes the ease and good fortune of the old mare to foal every year with no real problems. Medicine Crow hoped that my father, too, would lead a life of ease and good fortune.
>
> Then returning from World War II, my father was given the name Bird Shirt, a name of his clan. It is customary for a male to change to an adult name after the first participation in a war party. The parents, along with the clan uncles, are the proper persons to handle the transfer of a particular name change. Names like this one stay in the clan but they are transferred from one member to another as the need arises. It is not unusual for an individual to acquire several names in his life. In some instances, a person's name is changed if he is having difficulty in life. The new name will help him find himself.

Henry's explanation indicates the closeness of the Indians to their names and to their environment. In addition, it suggests that a change in name can bring about a change in fortune, attitude, or personality. This echoes the idea that words can change the way things are and offers another reason why the Native American chooses to use words in a responsible manner.

Indian writers frequently use metaphors taken from nature. In her poem "Red Rock Ceremonies" (Niatum, 1975, p. 164), Anita Probst demonstrates an ability to create striking natural metaphors:

> With low thunder, with red bushes smooth
> as water stones, with the blue-arrowed rain,
> its dark feathers curving down
> and the white-tailed running deer—
> the desert sits, a maiden with obsidian eyes,
> brushing the star-tasseled dawn from her lap.

Here, the natural metaphors include "red bushes smooth as water stones," "blue-arrowed rain" with its "dark feathers," "obsidian eyes," and "star-tasseled dawn." Probst's notable personification of the desert as a maiden who brushes "the star-tasseled dawn from her lap" reinforces the closeness of the Indian to the natural world. At times, Indian writers further emphasize that closeness in passages where the speaker merges personal identity with an object or animal from the natural world. Examples are abundant, but some are particularly memorable. In her poem "Indian Song: Survival" (Rosen, 1975, p. 25), Silko writes:

> taste me,
> I am the wind
> touch me,
> I am the lean gray deer
> running on the edge of the rainbow.

Silence as a Part of Indian Literature

Silence is the final characteristic of Native American literature to be discussed in this essay. Perhaps this concept is the most intriguing because it cannot be demonstrated with concrete examples. Nevertheless, it operates in contemporary Indian writing.

In an oral story, we recognize silence as an inherent part of the story. Silence may be used dramatically to build suspense, or it may provide a period of time in which the imagination of the listener can work. But in a written story or poem, silence and the importance of that silence are more difficult to apprehend. In spite of that difficulty, Charles Ballard, in speaking of Indian literature, encourages the reader to listen to the silence and what it is saying.

In part, the silence indicates the complex and highly personal relationship Indian writers have to their heritage and their society. This relationship cannot always be expressed in words. It is to be felt, sensed, intuited.

The silence of contemporary Native American literature also is one manifestation of the awesome silence that reflects the mystery of the Indian culture, a mystery that by its very nature denies expression. At times the Indian's approach to this mystery is through ritual or ceremony; but the concept itself defies articulation. To make a comparison with a concept from our own culture, we might reflect on the variety and intensity of feelings that are lumped together as love. Often love is best expressed in nonverbal ways.

In addition, the silence arises from the Indian's sense of continuity and the unity of all things. Imagine for a moment a great moving wheel that is touching the heavens and the earth. Imagine further that the wheel contains the mystery of creation as well as the ceremony, ritual, and "real talk" necessary to instruct humans and unify them with all creation. Only a section of the wheel touches the earth at a given time. Yet there is a certainty, given the cyclical movement of the wheel, that all sections will touch (or indeed have touched) at some time. We may infer from this that much is already known or much is to be known. In addition, much will be expressed through ritual and ceremony.

Finally, there is the power of the words themselves, and the Indian's desire to use them in a responsible manner. Those with a profound respect for words do not want to use them foolishly or unnecessarily. Indian writers tend to use few words; much of the intensity of their literature derives from this economy. Underlying this economy is the wisdom of knowing which words to use. At times a few will do when many will not. Underlying it also is the knowledge that much is already known. As the Papago singer says, "The song is short because we know so much." In the silence, it seems to me, there is the certainty that much has gone before and much is yet to come—the certainty of unity. Moreover, the silence affords the poetical imagination and the mythological understanding a chance to operate. The silence, in other words, invites the reader as listener to become a participant in the Indian writer's work and world.

7 Folklore and the New Student

Peter J. Petersen
Shasta College

Can James Doherty's ideal of egalitarian education survive in the mundane context of required courses, tracking systems, and placement examinations? Peter Petersen suggests that it can. Acknowledging the inherent problems of a so-called remedial English course, he presents an approach to writing that builds upon the students' strengths. Although the essay deals with an unusual subject matter, there are a number of general suggestions that may be useful for teachers who have no particular interest in folklore.

In "Three Ways of Looking at an Open Door," James Doherty proposes that the "new student" be educated as a person rather than as a plumber. Although I agree with the proposal, I see two immediate obstacles: the colleges and the students. Even if community colleges were willing to give all students the benefits of a liberal education, many of the students would be unwilling to accept them.

The English teacher who is committed to egalitarian education begins with several handicaps. At this time most community colleges still require students to take basic English courses. The rationale for the requirement is simply that students will avoid English if they possibly can. Most schools use some kind of test to determine which English course a student must take. The inevitable result of the placement ritual is a group of English classes made up almost entirely of the new students. Although school officials give these courses titles such as "Fundamentals of Communication" or "Communication Workshop," the students themselves are more direct. They call the class "Bonehead English," and they resent being there.

The classroom is constructed incorrectly: there are not enough seats in the back row. The new students want to sit as far from the teacher as possible, to disappear, to get through the ordeal with a minimum of pain. They know what happens in an English class. Students write papers about subjects that don't matter, and the teacher makes red marks on the papers. Whatever the red marks say makes little difference—nobody reads them anyway. But the marks themselves seem to be a special, coded language which, loosely translated, says, "You're dumb."

As veterans of English-class wars, these students have elaborate defenses against the humiliation that English class entails. The simplest form of defense is passive resistance. If you don't do anything you are in little danger of being embarrassed. The teacher may make you feel lazy, but feeling lazy is preferable to feeling stupid.

Another line of defense, more practical in that the student may pass the course, is to reverse the humiliation. Instead of allowing the teacher to make a fool of you as a student, you make a fool of the teacher. A few daring individuals will do this overtly, making ill-timed jokes or asking irrelevant questions. For most students, however, the reversal of humiliation is a private matter. Simply decide that the teacher and the subject are ridiculous; then you can do the assignments and not be affected by the grades or comments because you know that the whole thing is an exercise in idiocy. Figure out what the teacher wants—whether it is sincerity or wide margins—and give it to him or her.

All the defenses have in common a lack of involvement. When students become involved, they run the risk of being burned, and these new students have been burned too often.

The situation for the English teacher is not totally hopeless. Any approach that includes common sense and common courtesy will draw some of the students out from behind their protective barriers. As the semester progresses, some students will even pay the teacher what they conceive to be the ultimate compliment: "You're not really like an English teacher."

Partial success is no mean accomplishment. Certainly it is all that most institutions expect. One dean of instruction used to justify overloading remedial classes by telling us, "Half of them will be gone in four weeks anyway."

Folklore as an Aid to Teaching

But partial success is hard to live with, and anyone who works with the new students soon searches for ways to improve the odds.

My present approach is to abandon conventional reading and exercise material and to use folklore as a basis for the class. This approach is founded upon one of the truisms of teaching. I begin with the students' strength—their ability to use speech—and use that ability as a starting point for further work.

Providing a satisfactory definition of folklore is difficult. In simple terms, folklore is traditional material passed from one person to another by informal means. One person tells another something; one person shows another how to do something. It may be a riddle, the way to play a game, a song, an elaborate fairy tale, a proverb, a joke, a way to make something. In the more precise words of Jan Brunvand, "Folklore is passed on by word of mouth or example in traditional forms that are constantly changing within some group of people who share one or more common traits, such as occupation, age, ethnic background, religion, or place of residence." The groups within which folklore is circulated are called folk groups and are not exclusive. Each person is a member of many folk groups.

For the students, the most remarkable thing about studying folklore is that they have something to contribute. Each student has a personal repertoire of folk materials that is different from all others. No one else has heard grandfather mutter, "Foresight beats hindsight by a damn sight." No one else has had to experience Aunt Ethel's lemonade and honey remedy. Students are conscious of only a small part of their personal repertoire, but will recall many more items while listening to other people's materials.

The Oral Collection Session

A collection session is often chaotic, as forgotten materials suddenly emerge faster than they can be recorded. One student's story about the drunkard who falls into an open grave jars the memories of the listeners: "I heard that one, but there werc two guys." "I heard one like that, except . . ." "I heard one about these two kids in a graveyard." Each student's contribution is important, both as an addition to the collection and as a stimulus for the others. The teacher is only one member of the group, with contributions no more important than those of any other member.

Contrast this kind of session with a class meeting in which the students are to discuss an assigned story or essay. In this instance the students suspect, probably correctly, that the teacher already knows more about the piece than they will ever know. No matter what they say about the work, the teacher will learn little, and each student comment will be treated as a right or wrong answer.

The comparison is unfair and oversimplified, but I am concerned with student perception rather than absolute accuracy. In the collection session, no one is being judged. The class members are simply working together to compile materials. Free from any threat of humiliation and having something to contribute that no one else can, the student is in the unfamiliar but very comfortable position of feeling significant in the classroom.

The class can be student-centered in another respect. It would be impossible, in one semester, to study all of the areas included in the broad field of folklore. Recognizing that there is no obligation to cover the entire field, the teacher is free to let the students explore whatever interests them. A class may concentrate upon horror stories or children's games with equally valuable results.

It is not always easy to predict which segments of folklore will interest a class or which will offer the richest possibilities for discussion. A questionnaire, drawn up with the particular region in mind, will often help the class decide upon direction. Because at this point I am interested only in general trends, I prefer a format that calls for one-word responses: none, some, many. The form might contain such standard items as these:

1. Do you know any stories about place names in this area?

2. Do you remember hearing of cures (other than commercial medicines) for colds, headaches, hiccoughs, arthritis, or any other diseases or discomforts?

3. Do you remember any stories about college that you heard in high school?

4. Do you remember any ghost stories or frightening tales that were told around campfires, at pajama parties, or other such occasions?

5. Do you know any parodies (imitations that make fun of the original) of nursery rhymes or commercials? (Example: "Mary had a little lamb. The doctor fainted.")

These general questions can be supplemented with more specific questions about local phenomena. For example, in the northern California area where I teach, students would be asked to recall stories about lost mines, Bigfoot, the Lemurians, or about predicted disasters such as the collapse of Shasta Dam or the eruption of Mount Lassen.

The same information could be gathered without a question-naire, but the operation would be time-consuming. Whatever loss of spontaneity results from the polling system is made up by the clearer direction the class can take. Also, the questions tend to pique the students' curiosity, and the process often has to be inter-rupted long enough for someone to explain who the Lemurians are.

Developing Awareness of Differing Value Systems

When the class begins to share materials on a subject, inevitably there will be contradictions. The same mine will be located in two different mountain ranges; the same feat will be ascribed to differ-ent men; two entirely different and equally plausible stories will account for a town's name. It is crucial that no judgment be made. The students are compiling what they have heard, and the only right answer is a correct account of what was told.

This folkloric approach treats all groups with respect. The pur-pose is to study what exists, not to judge or to change. For the new students, this approach is valuable. The term *culturally de-prived*, often applied to these students, is meaningless to the folk-lorist except as an example of ethnocentrism. *Culturally deprived* simply means a lack of the elements that exist in the culture of the one who applies the term.

We are all ethnocentric, of course, and there is some value in allowing people to recognize their biases. A quick way to do this is to encourage a class to talk about Christmas or birthday rituals. As the Christmas Eve present-openers begin to gang up on those who wait until Christmas morning, with the compromisers (one present the night before) leaning back in their chairs, the students are learning that there are other equally valid ways of doing and look-ing at things. They also will be learning that their first reaction to these other equally valid ways is often negative. Becoming aware of ethnocentrism is the first step toward tolerance. Students begin to understand both their reactions to things that are different and other people's reactions to their different ways.

A more complex form of tolerance develops out of the study of folklore. As a class studies individual items (i.e., a story about an interfering mother-in-law or a method for water witching), one question continually recurs: What value does this item have for the people who circulate it? Or, more briefly, why is this told? Often there is no single clear answer, but the question of value will come up again, as it should. If an item has no value to a folk group, it will be forgotten or changed.

The function of a specific item may be straightforward. A standardized greeting may confirm one's place in the group. A proverb may lend the authority of tradition to an otherwise bland statement. A joke may confirm a shared prejudice or anxiety. A story may teach a lesson. Like other types of communication, however, folklore often works on several levels at once.

When I attended a rural community college, I heard several variants of the following story:

> A group of guys put a tomcat through the University of California at Berkeley. They enrolled it in big classes and had somebody who had had the class take the tests. The cat almost graduated cum laude, but a couple of the people taking tests didn't remember the courses as well as they thought, and the cat got some C's and D's in upper-division work.

The story was humorous and detailed enough to seem plausible, but its function for us was much more than entertainment. It justified our anxiety about transferring to a huge university, where students were so anonymous that even a cat could graduate. At the same time, the successful prank was a victory for the students, a victory over the system. And any suggestion that the system could be defeated served to ease our fears.

Looking at specific pieces of folklore, we are led to consider the values of the group in which the pieces circulate. Similarly, by studying the stories that we were told as children, we learn much about our own value systems and how they were formed.

Putting Folklore in Proper Perspective

It is probably time to remind you that I am discussing an English course, not a class in folklore or personal adjustment. The elements I have discussed are essential to the success of the class, but they are not the whole class.

From the beginning the students are exploring the use of language, even though they are working from a different point of view. Many of the basic lessons of successful communication are learned indirectly. The concept of the folk group, for example, helps the students to recognize that communication demands an audience—and one for whom certain kinds of translation must be made. The story that is immediately understood by lumber workers has to be modified when it is told to people who are unfamiliar with terms like "green chain" or "splinter picker." As they examine folklore in context, the students begin to see that the speaker is performing for an audience. The assumptions that the speaker makes about a particular audience determine the selection of both method and materials. By studying different versions of a story and discussing the context in which each version was told, the class can see how certain elements were enlarged or diminished to meet the particular demands of the group.

As the students discuss the performances they have observed, they often struggle to find adequate vocabulary: "It was like he *really* believed it, but you could tell he didn't." "When she told this, she was acting tough, like none of this stuff scared *her.*" At this point rhetorical concepts such as irony and persona can be introduced naturally. Students adopt the terms, not to pass a test, but because they are useful in a discussion.

From Oral Performance to Written Composition

After the class has analyzed a number of oral performances, a logical step is to examine the differences between oral and written material. An effective way to begin is with a live performance (or one on videotape) that is then transcribed onto paper. The students will immediately recognize that the successful performance is far less effective when the words are simply read. As they work to define what has been lost in the transfer to print, they are dealing with the strengths and weaknesses of writing and speaking. Then they are asked to work with the written document, trying to discover ways to recoup what has been lost.

The advantages of this approach to writing may not be completely obvious. The students are looking at writing in a way that is not threatening. They are simply trying to find ways to make the written piece as effective as the oral performance. Writing is seen, not as a sign of intelligence or status, but as a peculiarly limited form of communication that must be handled with special care.

Once writing has been demystified, the students are somewhat less threatened when they are asked to write. By tying writing assignments to the folklore being studied, the teacher can remove the most frightening obstacle of all—not having anything to say. Students who are involved with the differences between two versions of a ghost story may even forget that they are writing an English paper. The teacher's job is to help them discuss the ghost stories without reminding them that they are, in fact, writing an English paper.

Learning to Do Research

The collections and analysis that the class has done lead naturally toward research projects. I prefer to begin with a group project that will serve as a model. Students are asked to collect material on a specific subject selected from the earlier collection sessions. The class members bring in examples, both personal and collected from others, giving as much information about context as possible. Once the examples are accumulated they can be sorted according to categories suggested by the material. When the examples are classified, each student writes a summary of the process and conclusions about what has been gathered.

This research model of collection, classification, and interpretation is then used for individual projects. Usually these projects involve an area well known to the student—job, hobby, or family. Because students are working with their own materials and with a familiar model, they are less intimidated by the idea of doing research.

If my comments about the writing assignments imply a straightforward sequence, I am overstating my case. Each class creates its own order. In a given semester a student may do one individual project or several, ten analytical papers or none. It doesn't matter what kinds of writing the students do. What matters is that they do write and that they write something that is important to them.

At the end of a semester it is always hard to tell what has been accomplished. Some of the important facets of the folklore approach defy measurement. I hope that the students know more about themselves and their fellow human beings as a result of their work. I hope that the experiences of operating from a position of strength and participating as a valuable member of a group have improved their images of themselves. But, except for my own biased observations, I have no way to determine whether such hopes are realistic. What can be demonstrated, however, seems to justify the approach. If the class has been successful, the students should write more confidently and more effectively than they did at the beginning. They should have an elementary knowledge of folklore, rhetoric, and research. Whether they go on to other classes or leave school for a job, they should be better prepared for what they will face.

The folklore approach is not a cure-all. It may not be the best way to work with an English class made up of the new students, but it is the best way I have found so far. And if we believe that every student deserves the benefits of a liberal education, we have to start somewhere.

8 Composition and Moral Education

John Scally
Ferris State College

John Scally's essay meets head-on the problem of relating composition to technical-vocational education. How, for example, can composition become an integral part of a mechanic's training? Scally finds the answer to this question by looking to Lawrence Kohlberg's work in moral education. Scally suggests that writing can be a stimulus to moral development; and, if this is the case, then teaching writing not only helps students master a useful skill but also contributes to the moral maturity of people about to enter professions and vocations that carry with them a high degree of moral responsibility. Scally points out that activities designed to stimulate moral development resemble the methods writing teachers use to develop students' writing skills.

My interest in the relationship between the teaching of composition and moral education grew from attempts to justify the usefulness of what I was teaching in freshman composition courses. The cold eye that I have learned to cast on the world around me appraises with suspicion those who purport to teach "values" and courses in "ethics." I still maintain that very little moral growth results from taking a course in ethics that is taught like a course in biology or algebra or composition. But that same cynicism created a moral vacuum in my own classrooms—a vacuum for students soon to enter professions laden with moral responsibilities.

My students are typical of those in most community colleges and four-year institutions with technical-vocational programs: future welders, secretaries, cosmetologists, food service technologists, x-ray technicians, tool and die makers, mechanics, and body and fender people. In the world of work, these students will never write to change people's minds, and rarely will their writing assert an opinion or define a value system. Rather, they are going to be technicians whose writing tasks—if they have any at all—will be to assemble facts and data into some readable, organized form. For years I assumed that if I could teach them how to do that, the composition class had fulfilled its service and writing could be defended as a skill that is useful for success in the real world. Lately, however, the nature of the society in which my students will work, the nature of the work they will do, and the kind of training they get before going to work have combined to make me see that I must give them something more than just another "useful" tool.

Arriving at Fresh Insights

A technical-vocational curriculum is traditionally concerned with creating marketable skills. It pays little if any attention to developing the moral maturity of those who wield those skills. I have a special admiration for good mechanics. A good mechanic has a close, almost intimate relationship with ailing machinery brought in for diagnosis and repair. If a mechanic manipulates nuts and bolts merely to receive a paycheck, his or her skills will never reach the level of craft; for a craftsworker is morally involved with his or her work, if only to the extent of doing a good job for the dollars earned.

My class schedules have allowed me to teach many students in automotive and heavy equipment programs. Clever analogies between working on an engine and writing a paragraph became my special kingdom of relevance. Then, in 1975, the state of Michigan passed a series of laws to protect consumers from unscrupulous garage owners who performed unnecessary or shoddy repairs. The state government was trying to legislate ethics by imposing a code of behavior on a trade that in thousands of documented cases had indeed shown evidence of corruption.

The furor the Michigan legislation caused among the state's garage owners and mechanics reminded me of Clark's warning (in *Educating the Expert Society*) that the educational system was bent on producing a nation of "technical barbarians." And I was a contributor. I evaluated themes in terms of the strictly objective criteria of structure, syntax, spelling, and usage. I never stultified or influenced the development of personal value systems and ideas. To the contrary, I maintained a gracious tolerance for all sorts of opinions and ideas ("as long as you can back them up with facts"). After all, practical, useful writing demands objectivity; discussions of abstractions or assertions of unsupported opinion lead to "mere rhetoric," a skill irrelevant to the concerns and needs of my students. My most useful writing exercise subverted the freshman lament "I can't think of anything to say." But, I explained, writing is like building a chair: you simply glue and nail the pieces together and pretty soon you have a chair. Here are the pieces. And I would pass out sheets full of the "facts" and ask the class to assemble them, applying principles of unity, order, and transition to create a functional product.

Teaching people to manipulate facts and data to produce writing that eliminates personal involvement actively encourages the degradation of craftsmanship. There are all these facts lying around like random pistons, valves, and sparkplugs spread on the garage floor. Put them together and the machine will function. I was reinforcing the "scientific" notion of a value-free, mechanistic, indifferent universe, to people whom I would rely on to take a moral interest in fixing my automobile. Booth (1961) makes a pertinent observation: "When human actions are formed to make an art work, the form that is made can never be divorced from the human meanings, including the moral judgments, that are implicit whenever human beings act." In teaching literature we are compelled to talk about values and the quality of human actions. Why don't we do it in the composition class?

Teaching writing—by means of the strategies we choose, the comments we write, and the attitudes we assume—inevitably entangles us in moral questions. Nothing else in a student's education bears more directly on the development of a mature moral outlook than does learning about language and how to use it. The way a person uses language—particularly the interplay of form and meaning that is characteristic of written language—adumbrates that person's moral standards. If we can ferret out the moral perspective of a writer by looking at what he or she writes, then the possibility exists that we can stimulate moral growth through the teaching of writing.

New Possibilities for Rhetoric

The rest of this essay explores a perspective on writing and moral growth that offers English teachers some justifications for their profession and opens up new possibilities for teaching rhetoric. English departments seem convinced that survival means a parasitical attachment to the thriving, healthier bodies of the practical disciplines, so courses such as "Comp. for Mechanics," "Poetry for

Policemen," "Spelling for Secretaries" flourish. (One chairperson smirked, "It's still the same thing; we just changed the labels.") Ohmann (1976) remarks that ". . . even if writing were more useful than it is, utility of this sort seems an odd justification for a freshman English course." Why bother to teach writing to people who likely will never have to write anything and who can legitimately assert unassailable truths like "English won't help me bump out a fender"? Justifying writing in terms of utility is at best self-defeating and at worst hypocritical and insidious.

Recent research on the process of moral education has important implications for the teaching of composition. In fact, the work of Lawrence Kohlberg, based on some fifteen years of research, provides a model for a composition curriculum designed to stimulate moral growth while developing the writing skills of our students. English teachers have maintained for years that writing and reading patently help develop the whole man or woman, but no one has offered objective empirical evidence to support this claim. Kohlberg's research does it for us. My essay is intended as a door-opener—it gives only a sketchy summary of Kohlberg's ideas while emphasizing the importance of his work in justifying and validating what goes on in a composition class.

Kohlberg's Six Stages

Kohlberg (1971) specifies six stages in moral development according to the bases on which moral decisions are made. *Stages* seems to me an ill-chosen term because the process of growth is more like movement along a continuum, with each higher level incorporating the lower levels and being dependent on them. No matter how they are defined, the order of these stages is always the same: "The sequence represents a universal inner logical order of moral concepts, not a universal order found in the educational practices of all cultures or an order wired into the nervous system" (Kohlberg, 1971, p. 48). The sequence and stages of moral development (adapted from Kohlberg, 1976, pp. 34–35) are described in the following paragraphs.

Level I. Preconventional

Moral decisions grow from cultural rules of good and bad behavior. The dominant forces are avoiding punishments and seeking rewards (usually physical and hedonistic). This level has two stages:

Stage 1—Heteronomous Morality

One avoids breaking rules backed by punishment and is obedient only for the sake of obedience itself. There is no respect for any underlying moral order.

Stage 2—Individualism, Instrumental Purpose, and Exchange

The instrumental relativist orientation sees right action as that which satisfies personal needs and sometimes the needs of others. A pragmatic view of human relationships leads to a "you scratch my back, I'll scratch yours" attitude: a right action is one that is fair, an equal exchange, a deal, an agreement.

Level II. Conventional

This level is characterized by unswerving loyalty to family, group, or nation and devotion to an existing social order. This level has two stages:

Stage 3—Mutual Interpersonal Expectations, Relationships, and Interpersonal Conformity

The "good boy-nice girl" orientation results in behavior designed to please or help others and receive approval. This level is characterized by conformity to stereotyped images of "normal" behavior.

Stage 4—Social System and Conscience

The "law and order" orientation results in behavior governed by fixed rules and the maintenance of social order (doing one's duty and respect for authority). "Laws are to be upheld except in extreme cases where they conflict with other fixed social duties. Right is also contribution to society, the group, or institution."

Level III. Postconventional or Principled

The individual attempts to define moral values and principles without relying on external authority or identifying with groups holding these values. This level has two stages:

Stage 5—Social Contract or Utility and Individual Rights

The social contract-legalistic orientation accepts constitutionally and democratically agreed upon principles "in the interest of impartiality and because they are the social contract." But ultimately right action is a matter of personal values and opinions; "some nonrelative values and rights like *life* and *liberty* . . . must be upheld in any society and regardless of majority opinion."

Stage 6—Universal Ethical Principles

The universal ethical principle orientation defines right action in terms of self-chosen ethical principles. "When laws violate these principles, one acts in accordance with the principle. Principles are universal principles of justice: the equality of human rights and respect for the dignity of human beings as individual persons."

Kohlberg and his associates use a dilemma-and-probe method to gather data on their subjects. The dilemma is posed as a concrete though hypothetical situation demanding moral judgment. For example, does a man have a right to steal food or a drug to save his wife's life if he has exhausted every other legal means of obtaining it? Responses to such questions are analyzed in terms of the moral categories on which the judgment is based. Probe questions and discussion with others, some of whom may be at a higher moral level, stimulate and open up the individual's potential for movement to the next level on the development scale. People in a classroom will be on many different levels, so the interaction among the students themselves provides stimulus for growth: "moral stages represent the interaction between the child's structuring tendencies and the structural features of the environment" (Kohlberg, 1971, p. 42). The stimulus to change stages grows from conflict, and the classroom can provide the conflict. Essays, stories, poems become the vehicles for moral dilemma, and student judgment and interaction form the basis for moral growth. Writing is a way of communicating judgments and a means of revealing growth in moral awareness by interacting with the world of experience.

Use of Rhetorical Mode

Composition has the same relationship to moral development that D'Angelo (1975) finds between rhetorical forms and innate conceptualizing processes. D'Angelo validates the structure of what we teach; Kohlberg gives us a way of determining and evaluating the substance, the content, of student writing. The rhetorical forms are symbolic representations of the innate conceptualizing processes used naturally by the individual to recognize and understand the world of experience; in the same way, each person, regardless of social or cultural environment, moves through a natural process of moral growth that has close links to those same innate cognitive processes. The activities in a composition class can stimulate this natural process of moral development. If a student's writing reveals his or her dominant moral standards, we can help those standards develop and grow along with writing proficiency. The composition requirement takes on a new purpose: we are not only teaching a useful skill, we are contributing to the moral maturity of persons who are training for professions vital to our society.

That is a large claim. Is it possible to read someone's writing as a police officer reads a thumbprint? (Is writing an ethical thumbprint?) But if we can accurately identify a student's moral attitudes through his or her writing, then the possibility exists that we can develop writing programs designed to influence those attitudes. All I am doing is following hints dropped by some of our foremost rhetoricians. An example (Gibson, 1966):

> A moral justification for the study of rhetoric lies right here. We improve ourselves by improving the words we write. We make our performances less monstrous, by *acting* like human beings. Just what comprises a satisfactory human performance is every man's complicated decision. But, at least, by looking at rhetoric, we may begin to know more about who it is we are making believe we are. And then, perhaps, we can do something about it.

If we can demonstrate that writing supports moral growth, the teaching of writing needs no further justification for its social, political, and educational usefulness. The English teacher's work, in or out of the classroom, then takes on an expansive purpose commensurate with personal and social needs instead of shrinking to teaching secretaries how to spell. Writing teachers add to their tools a heuristic that can promulgate craftsmanship and encourage moral maturity.

To justify the teaching of writing in terms of moral education we must abandon the relativist, modernist position that reduces human action to meaningless gestures: everyone has a set of personal standards and can do whatever feels good. We cannot view social values as irretrievably fragmented and amenable only to some externally imposed order. The obvious question, then, is: What construct can provide a universal basis for our judgments and some pattern for the moral development we are encouraging? Humanists as well as English teachers are compelled to seek out universal principles of unity that reduce the antagonism between humanism and technology (or, if you will, between composition and usefulness). One starting point is to accept the premise that there are universal principles of right action, applicable to humanist and technician alike. This position is supported by Booth's (1974) convincing arguments:

> The philosophy of good reason leads us to a reaffirmation of those central human values that other philosophies and religions have reached by other routes: of tolerance, of justice or fairness, of "democratic" equality of vote in all matters that concern all men equally. Kant once remarked that the result of all his philosophizing was to establish a rational basis for the pious beliefs of his ancestors: the golden rule reappears for him as the categorical imperative, and it reappears in our rhetorical view as the concern to pay as much attention to your opponent's reasons as you expect him to pay to yours.

D'Angelo has suggested that teaching rhetoric develops the logical, cognitive powers of our students. Kohlberg's research shows us that, while nurturing cognitive development, we can also stimulate moral growth by attending to the substance of student writing. And what could be of more value and more service to the professions or to society than to encourage the development of morally mature individuals? In this way, the English teacher becomes truly interdisciplinary and can validate the form and content of the composition class with reference to a sophisticated body of research. Composition becomes much more than a useful survival skill, justified in terms of economic success. It becomes, rather, a necessary part of every educational and training program that prepares people to live and work in society.

Kohlberg (1971), following Dewey and Piaget, rejects the notion of ethical relativity. His research establishes that people in every society he has studied share the same methods of thinking about moral issues and the same pattern of moral development. This is a "natural" development of the capacity for moral judgment that occurs in every individual. Rather than imposing some external code of behavior or set of moral rules or "bag of virtues," the goal of moral education is to stimulate the natural development already occurring in the individual. The teacher does not become a moralist or a dogmatist. All the teacher need do is provide the opportunity, appropriate materials, and a suitable environment to stimulate the growth in moral maturity already natural to the people in the classroom. "The attractiveness of defining the goal of moral education as the stimulation of development rather than as the teaching of fixed rules stems from the fact that it involves aiding the child to take the next step in a direction towards which he is already tending, rather than imposing an alien pattern upon him" (Kohlberg, 1971, p. 71). What better place to stimulate moral growth than in a setting devoted to the organization and development of ideas through writing?

One idea occurs again and again in discussions of moral education and moral development. Kohlberg particularly emphasizes that the individual's moral growth comes about through moral conflict and "the precondition for a moral conflict is man's capacity for role-taking" (p. 51). The ability to see others as like ourselves is a necessary condition for moral development (a simple example is the difference between an objective examination of capital punishment and something written from the viewpoint of the man or woman on death row). Teaching a student how to change voice or create a persona thus serves a purpose far beyond that of manipulating or entertaining a given audience. "Essentially each of our stages defines (or is defined by) a new cognitive-structural mode of role-taking in conflict situations" (Kohlberg, p. 31). The conscious manipulation of the mask or persona in a piece of writing is, then, part of developing moral maturity in deepening empathy for others, and contributing to an understanding of the universal moral principles of justice: "the only 'true' (stage 6) moral principle is justice" (Kohlberg, pp. 62–63). The importance of play-acting and role-playing in teaching writing is a commonplace to the English teacher (one example among many is Dixon's *Growth through English*); but encouraging language play becomes far more significant when it is seen as an important condition for the natural process of moral growth.

Each of Kohlberg's stages, as he repeatedly asserts, represents increased differentiation and integration. What we try to do in teaching writing also involves differentiation and integration. Put simply: we try to get students to see details and specifics, to differentiate one piece of experience from another; then we ask them to integrate these specifics into a whole. It is possible, by the way, to speculate that if, as D'Angelo suggests, the formal rhetorical modes are rooted in innate cognitive structures, then the stage of moral development linked to these same innate structures logically manifests itself in a specific rhetorical mode. Stages 1 and 2 (preconventional) correspond to the descriptive mode: seeing the world from the perspective of the self. Stages 2 and 3 (conventional) introduce elements of cause and effect and comparison: the self is seen in relation to other people and to a system of law and order. Stages 5 and 6 (postconventional) employ analysis and perhaps argument—the ability to reach personal conclusions and rise to a sense of universal principles. As the processes of differentiation and integration become more sophisticated, metaphor should become more prevalent in a person's writing.

This has been a rather hasty tour through a complex landscape, but I think it shows some reasons for my belief that English teachers can both provide a "useful" service and carry on a tradition of humanistic education. I have seen composition linked to capitalism, Marxism, Buddhism, existentialism, and vocationalism—with much less basis than I see for linking it to the natural human tendency ("scientifically" validated) to accept and act on universal moral principles of justice.

9 Marshall McLuhan and the Humanistic Justification for Teaching English

Thomas C. Gorzycki
San Jacinto College

This essay, like the one by James Kinney, concentrates on the dehumanization of the teaching of English. Gorzycki shares Kinney's belief that current popular scientific thinking has had an unnecessarily harmful effect in shaping the deeply internalized values and attitudes we live by. The following essay calls for English teachers to consider McLuhan's *Gutenberg Galaxy* as a basis for recovering the humanistic justification for their profession.

Students who say they can see no relationship between studying English and their own interests or needs are familiar to most English teachers. A high school student once asked me how studying Chaucer could help him drive a truck, and one of my college-level nursing students evaluated my class by writing, "He taught me a lot about how to write rhetoric, but I don't see how that can help me in my chosen field, nursing." Both comments were lacking in sophistication, but each was worth more consideration than I gave them at the time.

English teachers have traditionally given two answers to such students. First, English has been defined as one of the humanities. Future truck drivers and other people study Chaucer, history, philosophy, and the other humanities because their experience of what other human beings have written, done, and understood as their purpose or meaning helps them understand what it means to be a human being. It "broadens" them. The second traditional justification for English is that it gives students a critically needed skill—the ability to communicate ideas clearly on paper.

The comments of my unsophisticated students were worth more consideration than I first believed because they were unintentionally attuned to a general change in consciousness which might eventually supplant these two traditional justifications for teaching English. At the purely practical level, most of us in communication have come to realize that ever since the impressive advances in communication through electronic media, writing effectively simply is not the essential skill it once was. Most people can handle their jobs and personal lives without the ability to write effectively. But a change in consciousness which alters the humanistic justification for teaching English is probably much more significant to our profession than any devaluation of an essential skill.

Scientists such as Conant (1962) and Bridgman (1959) may well have been the precursors of a change in the general consciousness that would have exactly that effect. Both conclude from their research that human beings have no sensory or mental apparatus that can approach an understanding of the essential nature of the universe. We can never escape our human reference point well enough to know whether our senses report an objective reality, and we have found contradictions in our scientific assumptions which make them all appear to be absurd. Bridgman concludes that human beings can only "shut up." As I understand it, this eliminates the humanistic justification for teaching English, as well as all other human endeavor. Since Bridgman concludes that as a human being he can never ultimately know anything except his own consciousness, his decision to shut up would nullify the goals of any writer, artist, historian, or philosopher. If accepted, his logical extension of egocentricity leaves no room for anyone who ventures to represent or interpret human experience.

Solipsism: An End of Linear Consciousness

Marshall McLuhan's "probings" into cultural change have given us the tools to see that such solipsism is the probable consequence or the logical end of a linear consciousness. Most people think of McLuhan as a media expert or popular sociologist. But perhaps his most credible writing is the groundwork he attempts to build in *The Gutenberg Galaxy* (1962) for his later prophesies of cultural change. *Galaxy* explains how our perception of ourselves and our world changes as our technology changes, so it is a particularly good source to look at when we think about how twentieth-century scientists have influenced the way English teachers look at themselves and the world.

McLuhan makes the fundamental assumption that we do have the ability to experience objective reality with our senses. In an ideal state, each sense organ assists the others to give an accurate account of what actually exists. He refers to the best functioning of the senses as a balanced "sense ratio." The combined result of all five senses working together is greater than the total of all the individual contributions considered separately because we have the power to "translate each of our senses into one another" (McLuhan, 1962, p. 5). This endless translation is an essential cross-reference which enables the brain to verify experience from its different sources.

Unfortunately, we do not exist in an ideal state that permits a balanced "sense ratio." McLuhan analyzes our predicament by using Hall's theory (1959) that each technological advance is actually an extension of our bodies. For example, weapons are extensions of our fists and teeth, and clothing is an extension of body temperature controls. In spite of the obvious benefits of these extensions, they create a far less obvious set of problems for human perception. McLuhan explains that "the price we pay for special technological tools, whether the wheel or the alphabet or radio, is that these massive extensions of sense constitute *closed* systems. Our private senses are not closed systems but are endlessly translated into each other in that experience we call consciousness. Our extended senses, tools, technologies, through the ages, have been closed systems incapable of interplay or collective awareness (McLuhan, 1962, p. 5). The effect of shutting off the cross-referencing or translating ability of our senses is blindness. Without the interchange among our extended senses, we perceive a distortion of reality. McLuhan believes that the twentieth-century mind is particularly blinded by an unbalanced sense ratio caused by its extensions. He says that "our extended faculties and senses now constitute a single field of experience which demands that they become collectively conscious" (McLuhan, p. 5). The blindness which McLuhan describes is a linear consciousness whose probable consequence or logical end is the solipsism of Conant and Bridgman.

Oral to Literate Tradition

In *The Gutenberg Galaxy* McLuhan tries to show how the move from an oral tradition to a literate tradition was a move from one kind of blindness to another, with a transition period of tremendous insight and understanding that we call the Renaissance. The perception of oral humans was so dominated by sound that they could not experience the constant interplay of senses that McLuhan considers normal. Today, on the other hand, we cannot experience this interplay because our experience of ourselves and our world has been dominated by sight ever since the invention of the alphabet and mechanical printing. During the transition, sight and hearing reached an equilibrium which enabled the explosion of insights during the Renaissance.

The move from the oral tradition to a literate one produced a big change in the way humans perceived themselves in relationship to their world. McLuhan quotes J. C. Carothers's article "Culture, Psychiatry, and the Written Word" from a 1959 issue of *Psychiatry* to describe the most significant characteristic of the preliterate, oral human. A modern preliterate African "comes to regard himself as a rather insignificant part of a much larger organism—the family and the clan—and not as an independent, self-reliant unit; personal initiative and ambition are permitted little outlet; and a meaningful integration of man's experience on individual, personal lines is achieved" (McLuhan, 1962, p. 18). The absorption of the oral human's ego into the larger organism is not a complete annihilation of the self, however. Carothers believes that a world dominated by sound is a much more dynamic, spontaneous world, and as such it is "loaded with direct, personal significance for the hearer . . ." (McLuhan, p. 18).

Literate humans reverse this attitude toward the self in relationship to the world. When we developed a written language, we also acquired the ability to freeze our sensory experiences into a static form. This static representation of our experiences gave us the ability to look at them more "objectively." But such representations were also far less dynamic and personal than the direct sense impressions which totally absorbed our distant ancestors in the present instant. When we learned to freeze a perception or an experience in written language and return to it at leisure, we acquired the ability to separate ourselves from direct experience in a way that was not possible before. Rather than being absorbed in the dynamic immediacy of experience, we became a detached observer of it. In the words of Alexis de Tocqueville, literate man "shuts himself tightly up within himself and insists upon judging the world from there" (McLuhan, p. 7). The logical end of this inward movement is complete solipsism.

Uncertainty of Objective Reality

I understand McLuhan's model of how human beings perceive the self in relation to the world to be a continuum. At one end are preliterate humans, so confident of the existence of an outer reality that they lose themselves in it. At the other end is the logical extension of literate humans, so unsure of anything outside the existence of their own consciousness that they become egocentric—eventually even solipsistic. McLuhan believes that humans suffer from different kinds of blindness at either end of the continuum.

However McLuhan evaluates his continuum, English teachers must find a place for themselves somewhere along it before they can come to a philosophical basis for their teaching. Walker Gibson builds his philosophy from the linear consciousness of twentieth-century scientists such as Conant and Bridgman. Rather than accepting the bleak consequences of having to "shut up," he pushes beyond their conclusion to ask what kind of response is possible to their findings. *The Limits of Language* (1962) is a collection of essays which Gibson selected because they "present a particular set of qualities and difficulties in modern expression." Conant's essay in that book, entitled "The Changing Scientific Scene, 1900–1950," must have greatly influenced Gibson because he refers to it extensively in his own essay, "Play and the Teaching of Writing" (1971). Conant says that scientists in the eighteenth and nineteenth centuries misunderstood the relationship of the individual consciousness to nature at a fundamental level. He believes that a faulty metaphor reflects that misunderstanding. In Conant's words, "Those who said they were investigating the structure of the universe imagined themselves as the equivalent of early explorers and map-makers" (Gibson, 1962, p. 24). But Conant believes that developments in modern physics have forced scientists to see the absurdity of this metaphor. More specifically, the results of many experiments demand that physicists accept the idea that, although corpuscular and wave theories of light should be mutually exclusive, light is, nevertheless, both corpuscular and wave.

Conant explains the problem this logical contradiction creates for the map-making metaphor thus: "It almost seems as though the modern physicist were like an explorer who, uncertain as to whether the colored areas seen from a distance were rocks or trees, found on looking they were both!" (Gibson, 1962, p. 27). Such explorers must conclude that something has gone terribly wrong with their sensory apparatus or that they have stumbled into territory so foreign that they can never hope to understand it, much less map it. Alexis de Tocqueville's linear man, mentioned previously, "shuts himself tightly up within himself and insists on judging the world from there." Conant carries his linearity much further. He shuts himself up tightly within himself and says that if an objective reality does exist, man has no sensory or mental equipment that can measure it. Conant agrees with Bridgman that contemporary scientists who accept this view of human limitation can only "shut up."

Education and Self-Creation

Gibson accepts the idea that humans can never know whether their senses report an objective reality. Speaking to English teachers or other careful readers, Gibson (1971) says "everything we criticize in the names of 'precision,' 'exactness,' and other such virtues, we do in response to an image of the writer as an explorer and mapper of a universe spread out before him for examination" (p. 281). Then he rejects the applicability of the map-making metaphor because he comes to believe, as Conant did, that the universe is *not* spread out before us for examination. On the contrary, final knowledge about its objective reality is completely beyond our ability.

In his attempt to push beyond the restraints suggested by Conant and Bridgman, Gibson replaces the map-maker with a metaphor more appropriate to his philosophy. He believes the relationship of the self to the world is better described in terms of a potter before a lump of clay. Material in an English class should be taught and judged from the belief that humans create rather than discover their world. This leads Gibson to attribute an importance to the self which *The Gutenberg Galaxy* describes as the logical end of the linear consciousness. The purpose of education becomes self-creation, and Gibson (1971) suggests that one of the main functions of English teachers is to offer opportunity for the student "to try out a version of himself and his possibilities without committing himself permanently" (p. 285).

Although Conant bets that future cultures will adopt a much more relativistic attitude toward science, he does say that other scientists might be correct in their guess that "the idea of science as an inquiry into the structure of the universe may once again become firmly established in people's minds" (Gibson, 1962, p. 28). Some English teachers never adapted their philosophy to the scientific attitudes represented in Conant's article, but they frequently express discomfort at being outside the mainstream of current intellectual activity. For example, in 1969 Benjamin DeMott published *Supergrow,* a collection of his own essays containing a speech he had delivered at a convention of the Modern Language

Association, entitled "Reading, Writing, Reality, and Unreality." It presented his own philosophical justification for teaching college English as a divergence from what he understands to be the general philosophy of the profession. Although DeMott thoroughly condemns Marshall McLuhan in one of his essays, this speech's use of metaphors of discovery to describe the individual mind's relation to the universe aligns much more closely to McLuhan's philosophy than to Conant's and Bridgman's. DeMott (1969) says that the function of English in the curriculum "is to provide an arena in which the separate man, the single ego, can strive at once to know the world through art, to know what if anything he uniquely is, and what some brothers uniquely are" (p. 143).

Education and External Reality

DeMott's statement contains several fundamental assumptions which are evident throughout his book. One assumption is that art does not exist for its own sake, but rather to teach people about an external reality. This also assumes that an individual ego can know of existences beyond the self. In fact, one of the essay's major justifications for teaching English is that once one makes these two assumptions, the old humanistic tradition for teaching English remains valid. DeMott (1969) says that English teachers and their students are elevated by "the extraordinary experience of raptness, selfless joy, [and] tranced involvement in the movement of a poem or story. . . . They are momentarily privileged to care for something beyond themselves; they are seeking to actualize (I apologize for the cant word) the range of humanness which flows from the capacity of men to investigate their own delights and to arrive at the mode of consciousness that gives birth to standards" (p. 139).

In his essay entitled "Exactly What One Means" DeMott condemns the zeal that poets have for "accuracy" of expression, particularly when they want to emphasize their own uniqueness by their precision. Gibson objects to the practice of judging student writing on the basis of accuracy because he has rejected the idea that language can reflect reality accurately. DeMott's condemnation has a different basis. He says (1969) that "people who insist on saying 'exactly-what-they-mean' are insisting on their own human importance, claiming a uniqueness of being, asserting their pride" (p. 133). In McLuhan's terms, these highly literate persons have moved far toward the logical end of linear consciousness.

They have become what DeMott (1969) calls "songbirds preoccupied with the one right word who lose touch with the Not-Me, with the world at large, a place never more exciting than now, never richer for seeing, learning, wondering" (p. 130).

Conant's bet is that in the future scientific minds will move even closer toward relativism and will concentrate upon the mind's ability to create rather than discover. In light of twentieth-century scientific evidence, he says that those who believe that what their senses report has some relationship to an objective reality must bear the heavy burden of proof. Clearly, that kind of proof is not available. In its absence, however, I believe English teachers will be much better off accepting McLuhan's explanation of how twentieth-century solipsism came to be so widely accepted.

If, as McLuhan suggests, solipsism results from a blindness inherent in the extremes of print orientation, a "retribalized" culture moved back toward the middle of McLuhan's continuum by electronic media will eliminate that blindness. Conant will have lost his bet, people will again feel comfortable with a belief in an external reality, and English teachers can rediscover an older, humanistic justification for their profession. DeMott scorns McLuhan for predicting easy solutions for complex twentieth-century problems. But even in his scorn, he retains his emphasis on the "not-me." As far as I am concerned, the great danger of twentieth-century solipsism is that it will produce English teachers who, like Hamlet, are paralyzed by an endless and unproductive introspection. Whether we choose to simply ignore the objections to the belief in an external reality, as DeMott does, or look for reasons to believe in it, as McLuhan does, is much less important than accepting its existence and getting on with the ancient business of offering English as part of a humanistic education.

10 Evidence for a Conceptual Theory of Rhetoric

David E. Jones
Los Angeles Valley College

This essay might best be considered a new apology for teaching formal patterns of exposition. Although most English departments implicitly require that such patterns be taught and most essay examinations throughout the colleges are structured on them, students frequently resist a formal study of what appear to be mechanical, static molds into which they must press their animate thoughts and feelings. Evidence from the work of Piaget and cognitive psychologists indicates, however, that the formal patterns of exposition are symbolic constructs of human beings' natural and universally developed modes of understanding and ordering experience. Aware of this, students and teachers alike can study composition as an organic, humanistic activity—not a mechanical one. And it is hoped that this paper exemplifies the constructive use of science, not scientism, in the humanities. [A slightly different version of this article appeared in *College Composition and Communication*, Dec. 1977, *28*, 333-337.]

In *A Conceptual Theory of Rhetoric*, Frank D'Angelo maintains that the rhetorical categories of definition, partition, classification, enumeration, exemplification, cause and effect, and comparison and contrast are "dynamic organizational processes, symbolic manifestations of underlying mental processes, and not merely conventional, static patterns" (p. 57). This theory is a timely one— in my experience, well-received. But for all its value, it does, as he says, raise more questions than it answers. Thus, D'Angelo concludes by stating the need for basic research focused on a suggested list of twenty-one points, the first of which is "the study of the topics of invention and their relationship to underlying logical thought processes" (p. 153).

What is still needed, to paraphrase Joyce, is that ideal scholar with an ideal insomnia who can fully correlate this theory of rhetoric to studies in biology, cognitive psychology, psychoneurology, and psycholinguistics on the nature of thought processes. D'Angelo has offered a firm theory, but until such research and synthesis are provided, those teachers of composition who might imagine themselves as one of Ronald Berman's "intellectual invertebrates" may find support in the knowledge that there is considerable evidence behind D'Angelo's theory.

My purpose, then, is not to relate the psychological and rhetorical structures as he asks (a task clearly beyond the scope of this essay), but to show that support from numerous studies does indeed exist, demonstrating the essential continuity of development from basic biological and mental processes to the formation of formal rhetorical structures. The actual evidence, in the form of countless specific observations and experiments, is detailed in the primary sources to which I refer. For the skeptical and the curious, the observations themselves can readily be checked; for busy instructors of composition, the conclusions and summaries provided here should be of help.

To me, the primary value of knowing there is support for the conceptual theory is that in teaching the formal patterns of exposition one need not apologize for forcing what often appear to be static, mechanical modes of organization upon the minds of students simply because convention and the essay examination require them, or even because they have been shown to be effective. Instead, the instructor can now have some increased measure of confidence that teaching the form and use of these patterns is education in the basic sense of the word—drawing out and up to higher levels of consciousness the most fundamental, universal modes of organization which constitute human intellectual activity.

The Work of Jean Piaget

Evidence from the work of Piaget and his collaborators can be found in many sources covering thousands of observations over the past forty years. Before relating their work to D'Angelo's, however, it is necessary to discuss some differences in terminology that otherwise could prove confusing. In *A Conceptual Theory*, D'Angelo refers to "innate organizing principles" and "innate structural patterns" (p. 26). This seems to distinguish between principles and structural patterns, yet attributes innateness to both. With this Piaget differs, but in a way that should not be important for rhetoricians, because his is a fine epistemological distinction between what is innate on the one hand and what is universally and naturally acquired on the other. In brief, for Piaget, cognitive structures per se are not innate, but they do develop universally as a result of one's interaction with the environment, controlled by those "innate organizing principles" that D'Angelo assumes.

Thus, classification and division, comparison and contrast, enumeration, and so forth are, for Piaget, "structures" resulting from highly complex developmental processes, not innate constructs. Nonetheless, these structures originate in basic organizational mechanisms, common to both physiological and psychological behavioral activities (Piaget, 1952, p. 14). This distinction arises from Piaget's "genetic" or developmental epistemology and can be understood only in view of the very basis of his system.

Piaget (1952, p. 1) begins his analysis of the origins of intelligence by stating that a continuity exists between the purely biological process of adaptation and formal mental processes. These processes begin with innate reflexes, proceed through habits and associations, sensorimotor intelligence, to verbal or cognitive intelligence. This continuity is established by a mode of functioning, a hereditary activity, which he calls "invariant functions," to be distinguished from "variable structures" (Piaget, 1952, p. 4). Because intelligence is for Piaget a particular instance of biological adaptation in general, intelligence "is essentially an organization and . . . its function is to structure the universe just as the organism structures its immediate environment" (p. 4).

The Matter of Structure

Organization and *structure* are the key terms for rhetoricians. The process of organizing the environment is the "invariant function" of all organisms. "Variable structures" are the result of this organizing activity (Piaget, 1952):

> The mistake has sometimes been made of regarding the *a priori* as consisting in *structures* existing ready-made from the beginning of development, whereas if the functional invariant of thought is at work in the most primitive stages, it is only little by little that it impresses itself on consciousness due to the elaboration of structures which are increasingly adapted to the function itself. This *a priori* only appears in the form of essential structures at the *end* of the evolution of concepts and not at their beginning. (p. 3, italics added.)

Structures are variable because they are developed through experience. From undifferentiated global generalizations, they become more precise as experience forces recognition of what should and should not be included in each particular structure.

If at this point we disregard D'Angelo's idea of innate structural patterns, and emphasize his concept of the formal modes as being symbolic manifestations of innate, "dynamic organizational processes," D'Angelo and Piaget are reconciled. What remains is to discover the specific origins of the formal modes of discourse in Piaget's invariant functions.

Invariant functions or operations exist within the framework of "the two most general biological functions: *organization* and *adaptation*." Although both of these functions are two complementary processes of a single mechanism, adaptation in itself is defined as *"an equilibrium between assimilation and accommodation"* (Piaget, 1952, pp. 5–7). Assimilation is the process of changing the environment to the needs of the organism; accommodation is the process whereby the organism changes itself in relation to the environment. On the biological level, for example, food is assimilated when the organism transforms the structure of food by chewing. Following this, chemical transformations occur in digestion. At the same time, the organism changes itself to absorb the nutrients, and the chemistry of the body is changed (Flavell, 1963).

The Process of Assimilation

This same process applies to intelligence as well. And here, though not immediately evident, is the origin of the elementary processes of analysis, comparison and contrast, classification and division, and illustration. Assimilation is itself a mode of organization: something in the environment must be incorporated, embodied, into some other specific thing in the organism. This presupposes, on whatever level, an analysis, a recognition, a comparison, and classification of what can and cannot be assimilated in any specific process. Notice in Piaget's general summary that assimilation applies at all levels from "sensorimotor intelligence" (from birth to about age two) to formal "thought" (Piaget, 1952):

> Intelligence is *assimilation* to the extent that it incorporates all the given data of experience within its framework. Whether it is a question of thought which, due to judgment, brings the new into the known and thus reduces the universe to its own terms

> or whether it is a question of sensorimotor intelligence which also structures things perceived by bringing them into its schemata, in every case intellectual adaptation involves an element of assimilation, that is to say, of structuring through incorporation of external reality into forms due to the subject's activity. (p. 6)

Piaget's terms *incorporates*, *structures*, and *schemata* suggest the extent to which he sees the organizational function of assimilation. How can there be an incorporation, a structuring, a building up of schemata, if not by analysis, recognition, comparison and contrast, and classification? Classification, in fact, is inherent in the definition of a schema as "a cognitive structure which has reference to a *class* of similar action sequences of necessity being strong, bounded totalities in which the constituent behavioral elements are tightly interrelated" (Flavell, 1963, p. 53).

The significance of this organizational process of schema formation for D'Angelo's theory is that the organizing function is innate and the schemata begin developing in the first days of life. Because the recognition of an object is basic to all organization, Piaget's discussion of this topic is important.

Initially, according to Piaget, the recognition aspect of assimilation is certainly not conscious; but it is evident that from birth the child, acting from innate reflex mechanisms (such as pushing, sucking, and grasping), begins forming basic schemata (what Jerome Bruner calls "enactive modes of representation") which are elaborated and refined with experience. These sensorimotor schemata "are not yet concepts, since they cannot be handled in thought and only come into play at the moment of their practical and material utilization" (Piaget, 1972, p. 25). Nonetheless, the functional similarity of schemata-formation and concept-formation is such that Piaget also states that "the concept of assimilation from the *very first* embodies in the mechanism of repetition the essential element which distinguishes activity from passive habit: the coordination of the new with the old which foretells the process of judgment" (p. 43, italics added).

Throughout Piaget's work one finds such terms as *foretells*, *origins*, *pre-concept*, and *pre-relations* which indicate the essential continuity of intelligent functions from birth through those mature stages of behavior that indicate the use of formally defined concepts, relational thinking, inference, and so on. Allowing for his cautious use of terms, the origins and continuity of formal thought processes are seen in his discussion of differentiation, which requires comparison and contrast of some sort, not initially of one object to another but of the object to the schema. As with all development, the process is from stimulus generalization to increasingly refined stimulus differentiation. Piaget (1952) states that from birth the infant begins with, among other schemata mentioned earlier, an undifferentiated sucking schema: "according to chance contacts, the child, from the first two weeks of life, sucks his fingers, the fingers extended to him, his pillow, quilt, bedclothes, and so on; consequently he assimilates these objects to the activity of the reflex" (p. 34). During this same time, however, "the beginning of differentiation" (p. 36) is inferred from the infant's rejection of all these objects in its "search and selectivity" of the nipple when it is very hungry. During periods of satiety the blanket suffices.

Piaget (1952) concludes this observation by noting that though there is no formal recognition of an object at this level, there is a practical recognitory assimilation which "constitutes the beginning of knowledge" (p. 37). He sees the beginning of knowledge, the beginning of psychic organization, in this reflex mechanism because of the "fact that sooner or later this act reveals a meaning, and the fact that it is accompanied by directed searching" (p. 38).

Fundamental Functions

Obviously Piaget does not discuss these functions in terms of rhetorical principles, but it is easy to infer that he recognizes the operations of analysis, comparison and contrast, and classification in these innate mechanisms (1952):

> The great psychological lesson of these beginnings of behavior is that . . . the experimental trial of a reflex mechanism already entails the most complicated accommodations, assimilations and individual organizations. . . . [and] if these behavior patterns transcend pure physiology only to the very slight extent . . . they nevertheless seem to us to be of essential importance to the rest of mental development. In effect, the functions of accommodation, of assimilation, and of organization which we have just described in connection with the use of a reflex mechanism will be found once more in the course of subsequent stages and will acquire increasing importance. In a certain sense, we shall even see that the more complicated and refined intellectual structures become, the more this functional nucleus will constitute the essence of these very structures. (pp. 41-42)

As teachers of composition in search of "underlying mental processes," it matters little if we consider these fundamental organizational functions the result of "practical" intelligence; what matters is that they are natural, not conventional—developed from birth.

Twelve years after *Origins of Intelligence*, Piaget comes even closer to the concept of comparison and contrast when, in *The Early Growth of Logic in the Child* (Inhelder & Piaget, 1964), a study of over 2,000 children, he says that "even at the sensorimotor level there is assimilation by similarity; it derives both from the perception of common qualities and from an elementary kind of abstraction which is intimately bound up with functional ends" (p. 283). Because this book is a study of classification and seriation, it is here, too, that we find Piaget's most pertinent statements on classification, division, and enumeration (Inhelder & Piaget, 1964):

> The origins of classification and seriation are to be found in sensorimotor schemata as a whole (which include perceptual schemata as integral parts).
>
> Between the ages of 6–8 and 18–24 months, which is well before the acquisition of language, we find a number of behaviour patterns which are suggestive both of classification and of seriation. A child may be given a familiar object: immediately he recognizes its possible uses; the object is assimilated to the habitual schemata of rocking, shaking, striking, throwing to the ground, etc. If the object is completely new to him he may apply a number of familiar schemata in succession, as if he is trying to understand the nature of the strange object by determining whether it is for rocking, or for rattling, or rubbing, etc. We have here a sort of practical classification. (p. 13)

Evidence from Other Studies

Piaget is by no means alone in studying the biological origins of thought processes. After examining evidence from every conceivable field, Lenneberg (1967) concludes that the biological basis of categorization is so fundamental that "all vertebrates are equipped to superimpose categories of functional equivalence upon stimulus configurations" (p. 331) and that concepts "are not so much the *product* of man's cognition, but conceptualization is the *cognitive process itself*" (p. 333).

Ricciuti (1965) has observed, in a study of categorizing behavior in preschool children, that those who had failed to respond to oral instructions for grouping certain objects would spontaneously group the same objects quite systematically while at play. Further experiments with children aged twelve to twenty-four months led Ricciuti to conclude "that these behaviors and their associated cognitive components represent, in some sense, prelanguage precursors of the more highly developed, language- and concept-related categorizing behavior of older children."

More recently, Nelson (1973) has studied twelve- to twenty-four-month-old children who not only demonstrated rule-based cognitive organization, but for whom "function or use of objects is a salient principle of categorizing behavior" (p. 28).

At the Harvard Center for Cognitive Studies, Bruner and others (1966) have duplicated and modified many of Piaget's experiments. From their study of "recognition," for example, they maintain that this type of discrimination begins at birth, and that it "is equivalent, in the formal sense, to the act of categorizing" (p. 103).

In psycholinguistics, the recent work of Brown (1973), Slobin (1976), and others has established evidence from thirty languages showing invariant universal characteristics of language development in respect to both structure and meaning.

A close study of these and related works will provide adequate material for establishing the precise relationship between the formal modes of discourse and their underlying thought processes. We have a bibliography. We have the insomnia. Do we have the ideal scholar?

11 Toward a Biology of Rhetoric

Arnold T. Orza
University of Connecticut at Hartford

Arnold T. Orza's essay shares the conviction of the preceding writer that there is a demonstrable continuity between natural process and rhetorical or verbal structures. But Orza is not convinced that this continuity is primarily logical. As its title indicates, his essay suggests an alternative term to describe the nature of the link, but makes clear that *biological* must soon be filled out by terms like *morphological* or *evolutionary* and, primarily, *metaphorical.* Michael Polanyi's word *post-critical*—probably the best contemporary term—accounts for the large role his thought plays in the course of the essay. In any event, the main argument has less to do with the problem of terms than with the thesis that all metaphor, in science, literature, and all forms of discourse, functions as a source of real power over the world of things and the self.

All of the National Endowment for the Humanities Fellows in the seminar that produced these essays share a concern about student writing, coupled with a weary but good-humored skepticism about the latest surefire "answer to all your problems." But we seem, nonetheless, to be stuck with a defensive position, with *trenches* and *barricades* being the dominant metaphors in our discussions. This position needs to be replaced by a renewal of confidence in the teaching of both composition and literature, and in language itself.

By that last phrase, I mean simply the belief that words are a form of power, useful not just to make a living but to make things live. The very students we seek to reach may be the last to grant us our conviction of the so-called interanimation of words and things, but that reluctance is the proper challenge to our powers of persuasion, i.e., our rhetoric. Students do not withhold this faith (which is what I take *confidence* to mean) from the languages of chemistry or physics, or even of sociology. This means, for one thing, that neither these disciplines nor their languages face the task of persuasion that we face. More important, this confidence in the reality of the languages of sciences is a measure of the gulf between literature and science, a gulf that makes our recovery all the more urgent.

Ohmann (1976) cannot discuss for very long the politics of teaching English in America without confronting the politics of the relation of science to English in America. Major sections of his book are therefore devoted to that issue. For the same reason, I cannot talk for very long in this essay about composition without talking about metaphor and science, even at the risk of seeming hopelessly remote from the practical and intractable problems of the classroom and the corrected essay.

Language Models

The recent crisis in the teaching of composition is a crisis not in basics but in the relation of scientific to poetic metaphor, and the answer lies not in grammar but in passion. That is the argument of this essay—that, and the contention that as long as we define the choice before us as a choice between composition and literature (or worse, between enrollments and literary criticism), no resolution of our crisis can be a lasting one. Not that it should be a function of introductory English courses to develop literary critics. Rather, a student's sense of the possibilities of his or her own language is best evoked by models demonstrating what other writers have made the language achieve. This may seem unfashionable, or even a bit silly, since it assumes a continuity between the English of Shakespeare and the English of today's new student. But at least it is democratic; it argues that a language belongs to all of its users. The alternative to this view deals with the condescension implicit in the idea that, while the poets may be proper food for those of us trained in more halcyon times, we have to begin today with where the students are "at." And we all know they aren't "at" books.

I have successfully and unsuccessfully taught beginning students for more than fifteen years and have just about given up trying to determine where they're "at" when I first see them. I envy those who claim they do know, but maliciously wonder if the expertise of the technicians who prescribe the cures for our new nonliterary student is not similar to the elaborate rituals of academic criticism for which the cures are a supposed antidote. Both agree, if for different reasons, that it's all too far above the sentence-fragment writer of today. A plague on both their houses! We and our students may just find ourselves together having to rescue a sense of the centrality and communal character of our language from the expertise on *both* sides of us.

I prefer the example of the comparatively uneducated and self-taught Keats (clearly the new student of his day—after all, he didn't know his Cortez from his Balboa) who thought he was not a bad reader or writer until he read Chapman's translations of Homer. "Then"—the word is his—he was so dazzled by the possibilities and awed by the challenge that the sonnet itself was his only way of responding to the silence of this discovery. As a teacher I am after that "then" and what follows, and I do not expect a sonnet. I'm not sure I even care anymore whether the student knows the poem is a sonnet. Yet I do not think I can get a student to share my passion for the expressed over the unexpressed response without supplying models of powerful language. Why compose at all, unless it can be shown that composed experience is a form of human power and freedom?

Student Skepticism

This question leads to the central obstacle to our, or at least my, rhetoric: our students do not believe that literary (or more specifically, metaphorical) composition is real or "objective." The following discussion of language is an attempt to answer this problem by proposing what may justly be criticized as a very abstruse theoretical premise for teaching composition and literature. But it should be regarded as no different from other attempts to insert the teaching of composition or rhetoric into the widest philosophical context possible. Even the Conference on College Composition and Communication feels compelled, in its controversial pamphlet *Students' Right to Their Own Language*, to locate theoretical support for teaching language and composition in the more arcane tenets of transformational grammar. While I share the politics of the pamphlet (as well as its suspicions about the political origins of the back-to-basics movement), I regard the selection of that theoretical model as an unfortunate choice. Transformational grammar is enumerative and logical, even antimetaphorical, in character and in inspiration.

How can teachers who expend so much love in getting straight the surface forms of their own rhetoric and that of poets and students find anything but cold comfort in the superior and generative value of the deep structures of those utterances? (I should remark here that the call of our NEH seminar to the twin concerns of love and rhetoric animates my search to replace this model.) I hope that at least a few other teachers will find the relation of metaphor to nature, both human and biological, as exciting and challenging as I do. I think it has profound implications for the teaching of literature and composition together, which I assess in the last section of this essay. At least it provides the intellectual support for meeting the rhetorical challenge from our new and our old students, that the forms of expression and the forms of things be one.

Metaphor's True Function

> Is logic the Essence of thinking? In other words is Thinking impossible without arbitrary signs? And how far is the word "arbitrary" a misnomer? Are not words, etc. parts and germinations of the plant? And what is the law of their growth? In something of this sort I would endeavor to destroy the old antithesis of Words and Things; elevating, as it were, Words into Things and living things too. (Coleridge in a letter to Godwin)

The purpose of this section is to think about language in an evolutionary and morphological context, i.e., to assess the relation of verbal form, as a function of and for the human organism (Burnshaw, 1970, p. 70), to other organic forms. This view entails a "natural" as opposed to an arbitrary (in Coleridge's sense of the term) interdependence and continuity between names and things. Language embodies the effort (most writers in the references cited in this article would call it the "desire") of natural forms to utter themselves in and through the human voice. Failing this, they would be condemned to silence and collapse. An example of this view is found in the poet Rilke's powerful images of tree branches bending into a lyre, or in the utterance "what stands printed in roots and long difficult stems."

Metaphor thus serves an evolutionary function while accounting for the process. It does not merely handle terms, as does logic, it *makes* them (Barfield, 1965, p. 70). In describing "the entanglement of subject and object, of psychology and natural history . . . of word and thing" in the language of the sacred Vedas, Barfield explains that language antedates a process of separation "whereby the thing is separated from its name" and points instead to a condition of "participation." "In the measure that man participates in his phenomena, in that measure the name is the form, and the form is the name." Or again: "The phenomenon itself only achieves reality in the moment of being named by man; that is when that in nature which it represents is united with that in man which the name represents." The "that" in the preceding quotation means for Barfield and others (Whyte, Needham, Sewell) the unfolding desire of organic forms for a fully articulated consciousness realized in human beings and by human beings in their language. In this context, metaphor is not a pretense of identity which logic's principle of noncontradiction (that A cannot be A and not-A simultaneously) continually undermines. Rather, metaphor is a medium of revelation and affirmation (in Polanyi, "indwelling" and "commitment") of the unity of nature and consciousness.

This unity is not simply or passively recorded, but promoted by the metaphor-making process itself. The word, to use the language of Coleridge again, is neither "that which affirms nor that which is affirmed," but the "living identity and *copula* of both." The last term is used by Coleridge deliberately, I think, to suggest the sexual as well as the grammatical character of the model he has in mind for the interpenetration of subject and object, word and thing. In one of the most neglected paragraphs of his "Preface" to *Lyrical Ballads*, Wordsworth, too, for all his differences with Coleridge, seems to have detected in the image of interpenetrated opposites a model for connecting the "direction of the sexual appetite" with the very "life of our ordinary conversations." Such an idea of language, however, runs counter to the view prevalent in structural linguistics—that language is an algebraic code and the ideal explanatory model is numerical. (Barfield calls this a sensation-plus-enumeration model.)

The problems and "nonsense" attached to seeing a logical principle as generative of grammatical and phonological forms would seem to have been pretty clearly spelled out by the mathematician who wrote *Alice in Wonderland* and *Through the Looking Glass*. But the dream persists. We may assume that certain features of words, since they share the property of *quantity* with other formal structures, can indeed be arithmetically transformed. (Sewell's *Field of Nonsense* is a spectacular analysis of just how far a writer like Mallarmé can take such an assumption.) A project of more valid scope, however, would have to keep these features integrated within a more organic and creative structure or "field" from which they derive their sense and which is itself reachable only through the creation of metaphor. "That which is creative must create it-self," wrote Keats, and his paradox applies here. What we are look-ing *for* is what we are looking *with*—the sources of verbal power are contacted and released in and by their metaphorical exercise. As I hope to show later, and as I think Ed Hancock's essay in this volume confirms, this premise leads the act of composition ines-capably and inseparably in the direction of poetry.

Such an attempt to bypass the divisive split into the language of science or logic (veridical) and the language of poetry (emotive) finds its counterpart in science itself. There is a continuing effort within biology to overcome the split between mechanism and vitalism as alternative ways of explaining the growth and structure of living forms, by moving to an organismic view proposed by scientists like Whyte, Needham, Arber, and Polanyi. With even its attempt at a basic taxonomy in disarray, biology is an appropriate discipline in which to observe the increasing demand for a more holistic mode of discourse and explanation. Like poetic or linguis-tic inquiry, it must deal with forms in process, i.e., transforma-tions. This accounts for the sense of connection between poetry and natural history in writers like Sewell and Barfield, where meta-phor is considered the language of metamorphosis itself. (An added dividend for teachers of language and poetry is the degree to which both the critics and biologists in the references cited in this essay locate their common ancestry in Coleridge and Goethe.)

So a writer like Barfield can astonish us with the suggestion that the objects of inquiry of the writer (speech) and the biologist (nature) appear on the horizon of being inextricably entangled. "Speech did not arise as the attempt of man to imitate, to master, or to explain 'nature'; for speech and nature came into being along with one another." The difficulty is that if biology can no longer rely exclusively on mathematics for the analysis of transforma-tions, it is left with metaphorical or mythological or "post-critical" accounts (Polanyi). Metaphor-making bridges this gap and unifies poetic and scientific composition. In both science and poetry, we seize the true and whole forms of things in the names we compose for them. All of the writers mentioned repeat this theme over and over again, and this essay could easily become a citation of their most eloquent passages. But three will have to stand for them all: Michael Polanyi, Owen Barfield, and Joseph Needham.

Polanyi (1974) attempts to show that the operations of science depend on a set of unassertable (i.e., unspecifiable by a process of definition) beliefs. This brings science and poetry closer together in the sense that metaphor represents the identical "commitment" or act of faith—what Polanyi also calls a manner of disposing ourselves—to the interdependence and "interanimation" (Coleridge's term) of forms and names, of nature and consciousness.

> We are faced here with the general principle by which our beliefs are anchored in ourselves.... The curious thing is that we have no clear knowledge of what our presuppositions are and when we try to formulate them they appear quite unconvincing. I have illustrated in my chapter on probability how ambiguous and question-begging are all statements of the scientific method. I suggest now that the supposed pre-suppositions of science are so futile because the actual foundations of our scientific beliefs cannot be asserted at all. When we accept a certain set of pre-suppositions and use them as our interpretative framework, we may be said to dwell in them as we do in our own body. Their uncritical acceptance for the time being consists in a process of assimilation by which we identify ourselves with them.... The tracing of personal knowledge to its roots in the subsidiary awareness of our body as merged in the focal awareness of external objects, reveals not only the logical structure of personal knowledge but also its dynamic sources.... An external thing is given meaning by being made to form an extension of ourselves.... These beliefs are transposed into more active intentions which draw on our whole person.... Like the tool, the sign or the symbol can be conceived as such only in the eyes of the person who *relies on them* to achieve or signify something. *This reliance is a personal commitment which is involved in all acts of intelligence by which we integrate some things subsidiarily to the center of our focal attention.* Every act of personal assimilation by which we make a thing form an extension of ourselves ... is a commitment of ourselves, a manner of disposing ourselves.

We can know only what we already are, but what we know *is;* we know external things only as we know our own body, by dwelling in them. They take on their living character, as does even the living organism of our own body, in our imaginative apprehension of them. They and the body are seized metaphorically, in the sense that we send our imaginations to dwell in them, and objectively, in the sense that things become the revelation of their own living nature. It is remarkable to watch the thoughts of men like Polanyi and Barfield work their way through the "mechanomorphic" (Barfield) phase of Western models for reality. Such models are outmoded now since they can no longer describe the emergence of superior organisms (Polanyi, 1967), i.e., they can no longer form the basis for a science of transformations, in order to return to an almost medieval view of the unity of names and things. "For the knowledge of the things that are, *is* the things" (Scotus Erigena as quoted in Barfield). And from this perspective, we might ask what role medieval conceptions of rhetoric might play in the shaping of a contemporary science of transformation. The possibility of a link between the two has already been faintly sketched in Sewell's *The Orphic Voice*.

The test of the validity of any method offering to reconcile rhetorical forms and natural process (as contemporary biology defines it) would be the extent to which that method retains the values of concreteness and of the body, respectively. Polanyi's notion of indwelling does affirm these values. It seems impossible to me to dwell, though, in abstraction, although I accept that a certain intensity of passionate indwelling could make otherwise remote abstractions come alive. I would simply argue that they then become concrete, i.e., they take on a body. Yeats said it better: "We cannot know reality, we can only embody it." So any view of the essential continuity of organic with rhetorical forms will probably also involve an effort to write a biology of rhetorical forms. How might such forms be systems of bodily activity, of the organism's attempt to articulate its inmost nature? Such a possibility is held out by the inspiring language of the preface to D'Angelo's *A Conceptual Theory of Rhetoric* with its talk of cosmic consciousness and the new rhetoric required for its expression. However, I think it fair to say that the book does not deliver its promise. But here might be a way to think about phonemes that could include, yet not be reduced to, the notions of the relation of sound to sense that are prevalent in modern linguistics.

> Those (who look into the unity of sound and sense) may find in the consonantal element in language, vestiges of those forces which brought into being the external structure of nature, including the body of man; and in the original vowel-sounds, the expression of that inner life of feeling and memory which constitutes his soul. It is the two together which have made possible, by first physically and then verbally embodying it, his personal intelligence.

And:

> It is not difficult to realize that these gestures (of the speech organs) were once gestures made with the whole body—once—when the body itself was not detached from the rest of nature after the solid manner of today, when the body itself was spoken even while it is speaking.

Barfield's writings are filled with passages like these, but it is one thing to assert such a vision and another to work out the assertions.

Barfield does so by taking a specific metaphor like *ruin* and tracing, as it were, its natural history. In doing so, he shows how the metaphor's expansion promotes an expanded acquisition of reality. The key to Barfield's thought is that he regards metaphor not as a primitive stage of thought to be discarded for a more rigorous and sophisticated logical phase, but rather as itself the more advanced and sophisticated phase. The most provocative passages in Barfield's writings are those in which he demonstrates how even supposedly abstract scientific terms like *cause, stimulus,* and *reference* represent accretions of this process. Thus Barfield, like Polanyi and Coleridge (whom they both acknowledge), refuses the split between abstract and concrete, logic and image, subject and object, thought and thing (i.e., speech and nature) by founding their essential unity on the metaphorical power that supports them both. Both the poet and the scientist are engaged in expressing the metaphoric (as opposed to mechanomorphic) emergence of organic growth and form. This includes, for Polanyi, the emergence of consciousness itself. And metaphor is the language of that account; the human "indweller" is at once the means and the end of the process which he articulates. "Man," says the poet Dylan Thomas, "be my metaphor."

Need for More Humanistic Science

In his essays and in his massive, multivolume *Science and Civilization in China*, Needham has defined the mechanistic separation of natural process and consciousness that has dominated Western science for three hundred years. Avoiding the errors of the vitalist position, he has nonetheless shown that only a commitment to a more "organismic" vision will enable science—especially chemistry and biology—to render an adequate account of the nature and significance of living forms, their interrelations, and their connections with human consciousness and language. In his scholarly work on China, Needham repeatedly limns the ironic implications for us in the West. His argument is that the Chinese have an idea of the universe as a living net within which humans are inextricably enmeshed, not just as observers but as participating organisms, an idea that frustrated scientific growth in China even though all the necessary elements were present.

In contrast, Western technological superiority derives precisely from the concept that humans are such remote and detached observers of the universe that they are actually able to manipulate it. Because we Westerners have now been brought face to face with nontechnological questions about the forms and processes of reality and their significance, we must once again regard the Chinese version that we abandoned. In other words, now that our technological advances in biology, chemistry, and physics have brought us to moral questions, we need to examine our science anew. Needham believes that China can help us because it has kept the idea of the universe as a living tissue of relationships and not, fundamentally, a machine. Otherwise, not even a so-called unitary view of the methods and languages of science, i.e., of the human reasons why we "do" science, is possible.

Like Needham, I mean to identify scientific and poetic and humanistic concerns, not to place them in opposition with one another. As one of my teachers used to say, poetry is a science, and science is a human activity, too. Aside from his marvelous essays, Needham does not specify the relationship between the language of a reimagined Western science and the language of poetry. Significantly, Needham shares with Barfield a passion for British Romantic poetry. From that perspective he writes about how our metaphors invite our recovery of the sense that we may participate in the living reality. (Incidentally, Needham's book on China discusses William Blake almost as much as it deals with China. One can guess why: Blake also had that view of the universe as a living organism where a mere "robin redbreast in a cage/ Puts all heaven in a rage.") And so we come full circle back to a figure like Coleridge, who knows science and poetry and language and can conceive of the universe as a detached collection of dead objects. It was Coleridge who gave us Westerners the alternative, complete with the same evolutionary implications that inform the writings of Needham and Polanyi.

> But man is truly altered by the co-existence of other men; his faculties cannot be developed in himself alone, and only by himself. . . . Hence with a certain degree of satisfaction to my own mind I can define the human Soul to be that class of being, as far as we are permitted to know, the first and lowest of that class, which is endued with a reflex consciousness of its own continuousness, and the great end and purpose of all its energies and sufferings is the growth of that reflex consciousness: that class of Being too, in which the Individual is capable of being itself contemplated as a Species of itself, namely by its conscious continuousness moving on in an unbroken line while at the same time the whole Species is capable of being regarded as one Individual. (Coleridge in a letter to Thomas Clarkson)

Application to Teaching English

What has any of this to do with the teaching of composition and literature on an introductory level? First it makes our concerns less parochial by connecting them to the general effort of our colleagues in the scientific disciplines to face the issue of the relationship of models (a term I take to be virtually synonymous with composition) to truth. At the least, this might mean that we should be in less of a hurry to abandon the interdisciplinary approach to teaching writing. This abandonment experienced a recent vogue but now seems to be in disfavor as departments of English face increasing new pressures to fulfill their "service" role.

Most important, it gives a radical new dimension to our invitation to students to read and write their language. We are not simply asking them to engage in an act of self-development, crucial as that may be. More than that, we are involved in the transmission of forms of power to which vital areas of reality, indeed living organisms themselves, respond—and correspond. This vision of words and things answering back and forth within an act of human imagination and expression, this living exchange of which metaphor is at once the record and the matrix, surely displaces the facile split of what we teach into subjective and objective modes of knowledge or forms of discourse. The universe disclosed to scientific inquiry is as invented as the inventions of the writer are real. The double helix and the myth of Apollo are, as Blake would have it, identified.

From this confidence, as I called it earlier in this essay, we can answer the protest of our students that the language and its literature "have nothing to do with reality." On the contrary, it has everything to do with reality. Indeed the very life of the real seems to depend on our passionate utterance of it. Apart from such a confidence, I would not ask a student to take the slightest pains to compose experience into an expressed shape only because the ensuing revelation of reality could justify its rigors. And by extension, I would not ask a student to bother at all with the expression of others unless I could show that their shapings were a source of real power too. Our students, and rightly so, want to be where the action is—and that is where poetry, like science, finally is. The value and power of assuming an expressed shape, insist the writers who are discussed in this essay, are exactly the same in both poetic and scientific composition. As the issue of desire, the vision of natural and verbal forms of reality waits upon the formulation of our rhetoric.

In this context the basics and the movement to get back to them take on their appropriate, diminished value. They represent the grammatical equivalent of the mechanistic aspects of living forms which can never add up to the fuller life of the total organism. Although those who urge the return to the basics speak frequently of a "decline," as if they also considered language to be a living organism, their view really entails a very static ideal, fixed and located forever behind us, in which correctness is the *summum bonum.* They really do not see language as a dynamic, living organism which can suffer "setbacks" even when being employed correctly and efficiently. I say this because I do not want to get myself in the position of being against correctness (I don't know anyone who is). I probably will continue to spend a great deal of time (as do most teachers of writing) in helping students straighten out the grammar and syntax of their compositions. But I will do so with no illusions; I find it hard to believe that anyone who has taught writing for very long sees the main problem as poor spelling and punctuation. If it were, we could solve it overnight—which probably accounts for why it is offered to us as the goal of teaching writing. We could quickly be successful with results that could be shown and measured. But it would divert us from the greater problem, which is less amenable to quick success.

That problem is what we should be about. How can we achieve writing that is concrete, impassioned, shows some independence, is attentive, hates abstraction and generality, shows commitment or, as Polanyi would say, indwelling? I despair less of making my students' impassioned fragments "correct" than I do of making their most correct sentences less meaningless and empty. Too often the model for so-called correct writing is anonymous, bureaucratic, detached, abstract, and demetaphorized—yet seemingly perfect and in full command of the basics. And we are probably implicated in the guilt of having built up and promoted such a model. I am not much interested in who the culprits are, but I do want to know what happens when we ask what's wrong with it. I do not know of a single issue in the teaching of writing that is more "basic" than the question of what will inspire and nurture the student's passion to write. I think the language itself can do that—i.e., the instrument will produce the passion for the subject and even give us an idea of what there is to care about, into what to pour our passions. But this language will be the one described earlier, one in which our characters (even if occasionally misspelled—for there must be comedy, too) are united to a living character of the things themselves.

I think it is a profound error to separate the teaching of composition from the teaching of literature. Simply, even baldly, put, literature alone gives language its full content. Apart from this metaphoric nature, any act of composition, including the simplest expository phrase, loses its meaningfulness. I remain unpersuaded, despite all the alternatives proposed, that a sense of what it means to use the language concretely and impassionedly can be acquired without recourse to the poetic sources of the language's power to make meaning at all. Poetry shows us language in the act of making things real and alive, and writers like Barfield and Polanyi identify for us that power with the desire of all things to renew themselves. In this respect, I am greatly indebted to the next essay, by Ed Hancock, for it is a brilliant account of how the effort to rescue the word and idea of "excellence" from abstraction and jargon takes him continually and inevitably to poetry and literature. He can spot the phoniness of the phrase because he constantly challenges it with the passionate care and concreteness with which writers make meaning of terms—with, that is, the living image that informs all real meaning.

When I can, I try to end my composition courses with William Butler Yeats's "Among School Children" because it is so totally "our" situation—the classroom, the students, books, reading and writing, the poet, and the terrible desire to make meaning in the very face of the futility and the mockery of it all. What I have been trying to say is probably reducible to the last four lines of that great poem. As he identifies the total organic form of a chestnut tree with the tree's act of creating itself, Yeats affirms the incarnate character of idea and image, of word and thing. For, of course, we cannot know the dancer from the dance; only in the act of being danced by the human body and by the imagination does the dance come into being at all. I guess we urge our students to expression because we finally believe that in speaking themselves they will create themselves. But I also believe that they cannot do this if they are too long separated from the general and living human body that imaginations just like theirs have danced into being.

> O chestnut-tree, great-rooted blossomer,
> Are you the leaf, the blossom or the bole?
> O body swayed to music, O brightening glance,
> How can we know the dancer from the dance?

12 Meaningless Forces

Ed Hancock
Western Nevada Community College

In this concluding essay Ed Hancock gives a personal account of one of the word-forces active in education today. He shows us the impact of one piece of educational jargon on our cognitive processes—and thus on our behavior and on the very quality of our lives. In this way Hancock's essay illustrates the central theme of this collection: the inseparable relationship between word and education.

When Joseph Califano was appointed Secretary of Health, Education, and Welfare, television showed him on the steps of the White House, microphones thrust before him, and brought his voice and "excellence" into our living rooms: "I want to bring a measure of excellence back to our educational system." A few years earlier, in the 1960s, educators throughout the country were reading *Excellence* by John Gardner, another Secretary of Health, Education, and Welfare who served in that office for five years. What Gardner said was that our major problem today is the need to achieve "some measure of excellence in this society." Still earlier, in September 1959, the Educational Committee of the National Academy of Sciences gathered thirty-five top educators at Woods Hole on Cape Cod, and the chairman of that conference, Jerome Bruner, wrote in his report, "We may take as perhaps the most general objective of education that it cultivate excellence."

Well, O.K. I'm a teacher and I've been hearing *excellence* for the last ten years and probably will for the ten years to come. But I don't know what the word means. Our leaders' calls for excellence remind me of that old military metaphor of generals, ensconced in underground bunkers behind the lines, telephoning through a bad connection their strategy to the troops in the trenches. But what's the strategy? What does excellence mean to the generals; to the

troops on the front lines? What are the troops doing with the word
and what is it doing with them?

A strange experience I had with excellence on the front lines
gave me a glimpse into several basic problems of language and has
helped me arrive at tentative answers to a couple of questions:
How noxious is the noxious misuse of language? What can we do
to free ourselves from destructive word-forces alive in our society
today?

How I Went Up That River

As Marlow, that sometimes reluctant narrator of Conrad's stories,
said of one of his inconclusive experiences, "I don't want to bother
you much with what happened to me personally . . . yet to understand the effect of it on me you ought to know how I got out
there, what I saw, how I went up that river." Like Marlow, I'm
going to have to bother you some with what happened to me personally.

I'd been teaching for some years and had heard *excellence* often,
yet had paid little attention to it. Education was riddled with
words that were used with little or no meaning, perforated with
*relevant input, meaningful output, innovative throughput, back-to-
basics, excellence.*

Excellence came in an educational Councilgram: "The minimum
of punishment is the maximum of excellence." *The Chronicle of
Higher Education* reported that the first agenda item for Ernest
Boyer, U.S. Commissioner of Education, was the "preservation
and promotion of 'educational excellence in terms of basic education.'" I flew to a state educational seminar with department chair-
men and deans of the college to hear an executive administrator
from Washington say, "We strongly support John Gardner's commitment to excellence in higher education: 'We must learn to
honor excellence, indeed demand it. . . . Slovenliness has attacked
like dry rot, eating away the solid timber of our national life.'"
We flew back. The deans called a meeting. "We demand excellence,"
the dean of humanities said, "from faculty, counselors, Learning
Resources, secretaries, and students." I left the meeting and went
on with my work as usual. *Excellence* was a nice, harmless, meaningless word. I ignored it.

Some months later I picked up a newspaper at a local tobacco
store and read that John R. Silber, president of Boston University,
was calling for a "compulsion for excellence" and in a "towering

rage" through a "stream of profanities" had told the dean of theology to "get rid of the deadwood—namely about half . . . the tenured faculty." The editorial said that Silber's pursuit of excellence had caused "dozens of students to weep. . . . And then there are faculty who weep, and the vice presidents who weep—in rage sometimes, in sadness others."

"Well," I thought to myself, "excellence has come to mean what 'glory' meant for Humpty Dumpty—'a nice knock-down argument,' but it is not so harmless if people are weeping and being fired over it." Still I felt quite pleased with myself for not having such good eyes as to see nothing at such a distance.

But then the distance narrowed. One day excellence walked into my classroom in the form of instructor evaluation forms carried by a counselor. I sat back, pretending to read *Breakfast of Champions* while a student distributed the forms to the class. I was being rated Excellent _____, Above Average _____, Average _____, or Below Average _____ in, among other things, "interest in and enthusiasm for teaching the course."

Gardner was right, it was being demanded everywhere. But this wasn't "our national life," it was my job. If I had been doing the rating, I would have given myself a somewhat better than fair-to-middling score, but not an excellent one. Not a lousy one either. I had known excellent teachers, six or seven I had had from grammar through graduate school. And I had heard about excellent teachers: Howett, Agassiz, Kittredge, James Harvey Robinson. How could that kind of excellence be demanded of me? Not even Humpty Dumpty, who could make a word mean anything he wanted it to, had that kind of authority.

The student collected and sealed the evaluations, preventing any duplicity on my part, and took them off to the administration. Some weeks later the results came back, sealed and stamped. I averaged out somewhere between above average and excellent, as did many of my colleagues. The dean called a meeting and said that he wanted to "assure" us that we were all "excellent, *exceedingly excellent* instructors."

I felt relieved, secure, confused, and a little crafty. Their excellence wasn't mine. But I'd accept theirs. I didn't know what it meant and I didn't think they did either. But that didn't seem to matter. They could demand it; I could achieve it. Even lousy teachers could. Students, teachers, administrators—we all lowered our standards, patted each other's backs, and went on our way.

Yet, without saying it to myself, I felt uneasy—partly, I think, because I had played the game and used the excellence that was floating about in education and partly because I was half-conscious of living with all the other meaningless words that decorated education—nonwords, ghosts with no hands or feet, no body, no substance. With words that sat motionless on paper or drifted off in sound with nothing above or below them.

But that is the way with words and people. They slip, shift, slide, change directions, reverse themselves, and lose meaning. Life is like that. So I dealt with excellence as I did with my thoughts about cancerous food additives and inflation. I shoved it to a small corner of my mind and ignored it.

The Dark Side of Excellence

Then commencement exercises came and my understanding of the word changed. At commencement I not only heard *excellence*, I saw it pop. Commencement was the catalyst that prompted me into open conflict with the word.

As we, the excellent faculty, filed into the hot, crowded auditorium, I wasn't in a good place in myself—that day I'd sat through two long end-of-the-year meetings about the end of the year, had missed breakfast, lunch, and dinner, and now realized that once again I was here at another commencement living someone else's dying metaphor. With a nod from officialdom we were seated, tassels and caps row on row, solemn birds of a feather perched on leafless folding chairs.

Then the commencement speaker, with what is commonly considered an honest face, a cowboy tie laced beneath it, spoke on excellence in education. The word gained force through its interanimation with the other words placed around it and the dignity of the speakers seated on the platform behind it. I heard only pieces and parts of what he was saying:

> And let me remind you that excellence is a commencement, as is this commencement. It is a beginning and always a beginning, never an ending. . . . This institution has encountered and pursued excellence in study, in teaching, in administration, in citizenship, in life. . . . Excellence is the watchword of the last quarter of this century. . . . The fate of our democratic educational system rests on it. The fine edge of morale and conviction of a whole nation grows out of excellence, viable and vibrant within it.

Under my cap I wasn't thinking but suffering a fit of brain fever. I wasn't prepared to sit, draped in a black robe, motionless on a chair, and hear *excellence* from above for an hour. I remembered Yeats's character Daniel O'Leary, who thought as he sat watching a poorly acted stage play one night:

> What would happen if I were to take off my boots, and fling one at Mr. . . . Could I give my future life such settled purpose that the act would take its place, not among whims, but among forms of intensity? . . . "You have not the courage," I said, speaking in a low voice. "I have," I said, and began unlacing my boots.

Maybe O'Leary had the courage; I didn't. Such an act would only serve to drop my near-excellent rating to dismissal, a form of intensity I was not prepared for. And who, I asked myself, do you think you are to indulge yourself in such superior conceits, the mockingbird, the make-bate, the malcontent, the sad, bad guest who cannot stand to take part in a harmless commencement?

My fever increasing, I tried putting a few positive thoughts up against the negative ones: Doesn't the institution, the state who pays me, have the simple right to require me, as Thorstein Veblen observed, "to expend time and means in such polite observances, spectacles and quasi-learned exhibitions as are presumed to enhance the prestige of the university"?

And why am I getting so precious about excellence? I know what it means. We all know what it means—do a good job, the best and better, excel, surpass. And don't we need value concepts for which we can sacrifice ourselves: progress, equality, liberty, fraternity? Why not excellence?

The speaker's voice was flat. The noises he made didn't carry any meaning for me. He was reading from the lectern:

> Our way of life depends on our unswerving allegiance to excellence. We must savor, not smother, excellence and continue to prepare ourselves for the continuing commencement of our attainment of it. . . . As I have said, *excellence* means many different things to many different people, and our democratic system of education now finds itself at the crossroads of excellence and degeneration. This is the danger that is the peril now threatening our civilization.

With one hand he made a sweeping gesture over the heads of the audience, then quickly tightened the knot on his tie.

The auditorium was stifling. My nerves were frayed. My attempts at allopathy weren't working. Reacting to the speaker, then reacting to my reaction, then to that reaction—I was feeling sick of something other than excellence and the commencement exercise. The word seemed to have worked its way inside my brain case. I looked at the faces below the caps, along the row I was sitting in. They looked bored. No, they looked unborable. I was coming to the limits of my feelings.

To be excellent is to act. This is the global truth. "What's he talking about?" I asked myself. But then he began saying some words I knew:

> mountain ridges . . . climbing . . . snow-capped . . . pure mountain air . . . aeries . . . tossed out of the nest . . . eagles . . . flying above the mountain. . . .

Head down, reading from his notes, he was pointing his finger to the speckled ceiling of the auditorium above us.

> Excellence, not complacency. Excellence, not rhetoric is your accomplishment. You envisioned excellence. You pursued it. You achieved it.

At about this time something happened that I didn't understand until some months later. At the time it wasn't clear to me what had happened—not clear at all. All I knew then was the *excellence* popped—popped in the perceiving part of my brain.

I had slipped back the sleeve of my gown to look at the hard facts of the hands of my watch. When I looked up at the lectern again, I saw excellence from the other side of the hedge, from the other psychological side of it, or more exactly, I suppose, from this side of it. Maybe you have seen that visual puzzle, the Necker cube? When you first look at the cube, the corner marked X appears to be on the front side. But if you continue to stare at the cube, something pops in the perceiving part of your brain and the X side jumps—or rather, you abruptly discover that your eye had jumped the X side, from the front of the cube to the back of the cube, and from the back of the cube to the front, inside your brain, without your having seen it.

Excellence popped and instantly pictures from literature passed before my eyes. As correlatives for my vague feelings, I suppose. No, not as correlatives, but as something implied, as something thrust on the mind through some unseen association.

I hadn't read *Heart of Darkness* for years. But now I heard voices and saw Kurtz, an emissary of progress, taking his splendid monologues on love and justice into a distant outpost in the heart of Africa, and there committing monstrous atrocities against the natives. I saw him with his burning, noble words, with his moving appeals to every altruistic sentiment—and with the heads of natives drying on stakes under his window.

And here at the lectern—his finger still pointing to the ceiling, without action, without Kurtz's passion, without candor, without conviction, without extremity, without a glimpse of truth, full of pronouncements, like a dying vibration of one immense jaber, silly, sordid, or simply mean, without any kind of sense—a voice. A voice.

And then I got a glimpse of Henry James's John Marcher, wading through the beaten grass, where no life stirred, looking for what he didn't know, the Beast of his own egotism. And not seeing it because he looked out for it through the very eyeholes of the Beast.

Other images passed rapidly before me. One of them: birds falling dead after preying on unburied human bodies at the plague of Athens. Another: Joyce's Gabriel hearing the snow falling on the treeless hills, softly falling on the lonely churchyard, on the barren thorns, the snow falling faintly through the universe and faintly falling, upon all the living and the dead.

From this it may seem that I'm overly fanciful. But I have seen no visions in my life. I'm nearly always in agreement with my colleagues on what is taken for real and what only seems to be. I'm not an unknown citizen, though I do buy a paper every day, am fully insured, have the right number of children for a parent of my generation, and am able to satisfy my employer. Too steadily, I suppose, I recognize my limits. But with little sleep, no food, nothingness from above and efforts to resist it from within for over an hour, and with two solid semesters of basics, comma splices, fragments, subject/verb agreement still with me, I saw pictures.

The speaker had stopped. We were filing down the aisle.

I got a sandwich at a restaurant and then walked aimlessly through the streets wondering about excellence and the images I had seen: burning, noble words and atrocities. A man unable to see what he is looking for because he is seeing with the very thing he is looking for. Birds of prey, dying. And then the snow falling, faintly falling on us all. I was puzzled. What had happened?

After breakfast the next morning, I knew one thing for sure—imagination feeds on hunger. And another thing not so sure—that I had seen something. *Excellence* had popped. But from what to what?

The Silent Scream in Our Jargon

One thing was now certain to me: I was in conflict with *excellence*. I had never been in conflict with a word before. Especially a meaningless one. But *excellence* had become more than a half-conscious irritation I could simply push into the background. Though I did try doing just that: *excellence* rose up from my breakfast newspaper, came to me on memos, confronted me in the hallway, presented itself at department meetings. I looked the other way, pretended to be hard of hearing, walked around it, turned my back on it. Yet sometimes I would hear "democracy" or "freedom," "equality," "prosperity," "progress," "love," "peace," "justice," "back-to-basics," "accountability," "criteria performance," and some picture would rise up before me.

"Back-to-basics," the dean said, and a bird wet its beak in the plague, clack, clack, and died.

The outcome was that during office hours, feet propped up on my desk, I found myself reading books about words and their ways. I wanted an explanation for the images I'd seen. In graduate school my "area" had been nineteenth-century prose fiction. Semantics was a field as foreign to me as neurophysiology. So I began by simply trying to pin a name on excellence. I wanted to call it something. What kind of misuse was it? What did the people who studied words call this sort of thing?

I soon discovered that we have a lot of words for meaningless words: *jargon, euphemism, doublespeak, balderdash, linguistic pollution, gobbledygook, unlanguage, duckspeak, no speak, sponge words, coxcombries, the fallacy of reification, the B.S. factor, cant, verbal card-stacking, public lying, dishonest language, linguistic sludge, twaddle, the language of self-deception, the emphatic fallacy, semantic distortion, marshmallow prose, Prosa Nostra, pseudocommunication, phatic communion, registers, gibberish, code-switching, Zieglerrata, baffle-gab, verbiageration, counter-attitudinal advocacy.* The words seemed about as vague and meaningless as the words they described.

There had been a plethora of such words within just the last few years. "Why?" I asked.

Students of language have observed that when a cultural need arises a language develops words to fill that need. The Polynesians have many words to describe the different stages of development of coconuts. Eskimos have terms for flying snow, falling snow, slush snow, hard snow. Clearly, I reasoned, the Polynesians have a lot of coconuts, the Eskimos much snow, and we an abundance of misused language. But it seemed our many terms for the misuse of language had not helped much. Misuse continues and the words describing that activity multiply.

At first appearance it seemed that the answer lay in more precise terminology. "But say," I thought to myself, "that someone did give precise definitions of the many terms we have for the various misuses of language. Wouldn't such an effort perhaps create a still deeper fog bank of verbal abstractions? Wouldn't the upshot of it perhaps be that we would feel more secure with misuses because someone had managed to set down precise names for them?"

Nevertheless, I found a definition that worked for me. Ivor Brown had noted that *jargon* came to us from France as a "pleasing warbling of birds," that the idea of "a warble wilted" and jargon became a "tuneless twittering, the sparrows [taking] over from the songster," that "Oxford gives the date 1643 to the appearance of jargon as 'a barbarous, rude or debased variety of speech,'" and that later "as a term of contempt it was applied to the language of scholars, the terminology of a science or . . . profession."

I looked at what other writers said about jargon words. For Raoul de Roussy de Sales, *love* is a word that Americans want to get "as much enjoyment, comfort, safety and general sense of satisfaction from, as one gets out of a well balanced diet or a good plumbing installation." A jargon expert like Donald Hall might say the word is "tricky false in its enthusiasm . . . a black ink squirting cuttlefish." Walker Gibson would say that it wasn't the cuttlefish but the voice behind it that was bothering me because I felt an "insupportable gap between myself and the person I was being asked to be." Richard Ohmann might see in *excellence* and the words accompanying it the "use of syntax to posit certainty where none exists . . . by a simple act of reification." Excellence was not a person or thing. It could not be demanded as could a corpus delicti or a glass of milk, even if we were all acting as if it could.

Though I now knew more about jargon than I had, none of this helped me much in understanding the pictures I had seen at commencement. What I wanted to know was, where is jargon bred? Didn't the pictures I had seen spring from a reaction or insight I had had into the psychology of the commencement speaker?

I tried understanding the pictures from the point of view of the logical semanticists. Words are embedded in statements and statements are used primarily in two ways: to refer to a thing or an idea, or to express or arouse feelings. Language may be either "referential" or "emotive," it may be used either to designate some object or thought, or to express feeling. When our dean said, "You are all excellent teachers," I wasn't hearing a verifiable statement, only feelings. The dean was emoting. The words were pure phatic communion: their meaning lay only in the emotion of their noise.

When the commencement speaker said to us, "You envisioned excellence. You pursued it. You achieved it," he was saying, "I am a good person. My thoughts and feelings soar to high things in the clear air above snow-capped mountain peaks. I think you're great. Think of me as I do of you. Vote for me next fall." He was simply expressing his wishes, hopes, desires, or perhaps fears, under the guise of what appeared to be verifiable statement.

So here was a politician, campaigning with a commencement speech on excellence. What had I expected? Gold watches? Objective truth? All I needed was a little peasant wit to know that he was saying: "I like you, please think well of me."

But how did his attitude, if this was it, call up in my mind's eye heads drying on stakes, birds of prey feeding on the dead bodies of plague victims, the snow falling on all the living and the dead? I once again considered the possibility that at commencement I had simply gone somewhat temporarily mad and had not actually seen anything. But that wasn't right.

I decided to keep digging. I turned to a scientific semanticist, to psycholinguists and cognitive psychologists. I was hot on the trail.

At Harvard Medical School, Eric Lenneberg, attempting to determine the psychological basis of purpose and consciousness, concluded, after studying neurons and supportive cells within the brain case, that "words tag the process by which the species deals cognitively with its environment."

Excellence tagged a cognitive process!

I rushed to the library late one night to read the Russian cognitive psychologist Lev Vygotsky, who had discovered basic elements in the interaction of cognition and language: thought, meaning, inner speech (silent inner-talk to oneself), and external, verbalized speech. These elements interanimated in one dynamic, living activity— but only when the mind functioned properly. Vygotsky also noted that the transition from thought to speech is no easy matter. Blockage may occur at any point in this living activity. With blockage, no thought. And a word devoid of thought is "a dead thing."

If, when the commencement speaker said *excellence*, the cognitive process had been blocked somewhere in the process of interaction of thought and speech, then the word he spoke was a dead thing. It followed that his cognition was also a dead thing. And, also, because word affects thought, those dead noises he made when he said *excellence* might then set up dead cognitive processes in anyone who heard them. Was it possible for a commencement speaker to dry heads on stakes?

Perhaps I am doing some forcing to make the commencement pictures fit the ideas I was now discovering—but not much, I think. At commencement I had seen something similar to what the semanticists were now telling me. Dead words were falling like snow, faintly falling through the auditorium, through our world, faintly falling on all the living and the dead. We looked out at dead words through our eyeholes, not seeing the emptiness coming in and going out as easily as our breath.

Now I understood what *excellence* had popped from on the front side of the Necker cube and what it had popped to on the back side. *Excellence* on the front side was an irritating yet essentially harmless misuse of the language; or, less harmless, it was a piece of jargon that might cause students and faculty to weep and people to lose their jobs.

But *excellence* on the back side was much more than this. Here was the destructive element in human emotions and the dead thing blocking consciousness in the brain. Here was an essential element in the makeup of human beings, the seed of destruction within us.

The front side of *excellence* I understood with the verbal-intellectual part of my mind. The back side I saw with the simultaneous, intuitive, part of my mind. And what I saw with the intuitive part, because I couldn't explain that part using the verbal part, prompted me to metaphor, to grasping for equivalences in pictures from literature. The pictures changed the direction of the whole current of my thinking about excellence—and all other charismatic words like it. On the back side of any of the big, meaningless words one might see the terror of the situation.

Like the modern physicist's atom, words are not things, but symbols, concepts, notional models created by the human. The structure of mind and matter and theory are not very different from one another. And words and mind and thought do not differ greatly. The observer is the observed. We are very much like our word-symbols.

So if one wet one's beak in dead words, then, like a bird feeding on the plague, one might go clack, clack and the life in one's brain case might die. And education was feeding on excellence from coast to coast. Feeding on *back-to-basics*, on *relevance* and many more—all words that were used most of the time with little or no thought behind them. And new dead words were coming along every day. The snow was falling everywhere. I now understood what I had seen at commencement.

Consciousness-raising: The Way to Combat Powerful Words

But months later I found myself still thinking about excellence. I had received a one-year National Endowment for the Humanities Fellowship and gone off across the country to Amherst, Massachusetts. There I picked up the *Boston Globe* in a local tobacco store and read about students and vice presidents weeping over excellence at Boston University, and there I happened across the Necker cube and saw in it an analogy for my experience with excellence.

"Can't something be done?" I asked myself. "Are we helpless before our words?"

"Well," I said, still talking with myself, "couldn't a lot of damaging words be stopped at their source?"

Back in 1959, when Bruner and those thirty-five top educators met at Woods Hole and said that the object of education is to "cultivate excellence," what did they mean? In the chairman's report of that conference, *excellence* meant "educate each student to his optimum intellectual development . . . emphasize the structure of a subject . . . devise materials that will challenge superior students while not destroying the confidence and will-to-learn of those who are less fortunate . . . use aids in teaching, the film or television."

I think it is too bad that the Woods Hole conference used such a vague, powerful word as *excellence* to stand for these ideas. Someone at the conference might have stopped *excellence* at that point. It is possible, however, for influential people in high positions to double check their words, making sure they use potentially powerful words only when they are given clearly defined referents. But it is difficult for people to be influential without using vague, influential words.

What had Gardner meant in 1961 when he said he wanted to achieve "a measure of excellence"? He meant "toning up a whole society, bringing a whole people to that fine edge of morale and conviction and zest that makes for greatness."

Yes, but is there anything more in these large, positive words than feelings intended to arouse feelings? And isn't it so, that to the extent to which idealism is illusory, to the extent that it flies off to bring "a whole people to the fine edge of morale," off above snow-capped mountain peaks high above human limitations—to that extent it will very likely turn into its opposite?

But say some people in high places do throttle some of the dangerous words at their source. What about the ones that get through?

Couldn't I, couldn't we, do something about them once they come to us? Couldn't we re-create the words, giving them personal meaning by experiencing them on the personal level? As Richard Weaver has said, "Perhaps the best that any of us can do is to hold a dialectic with himself to see what the wider circumferences of his terms of persuasion are. The process will . . . prevent his becoming a creature of evil public forces and a victim of his own thoughtless rhetoric." A sure solution, but dialectics with oneself aren't for everyone.

Why not put the educational system to work, educating people to the potential violence in word-forces? Vaccinate all students with required courses in semantics. Or better yet, inoculate them with frequent injections of good poetry and good literature until the vivid, concrete detail of words with meaning moves through their veins, making them immune to meaningless jargon.

But is this possible? The country is in the grip of a back-to-basics movement, and whatever that means, it does not mean good literature.

Perhaps we could organize a team of trained word-watchers who, like bird-watchers, would not observe stuffed specimens in the laboratory but would go into the field equipped with binoculars and sketch pads and, through painstaking observation of words in flight, compile a short, clear *Field Guide to Contemporary Word-Forces*? Would not such a guide, in the hands of people directly and indirectly affected by the use of particular words, do a lot of good?

I'm convinced that if public officials, administrators, deans, teachers, and students throughout the country had such a field guide in their hands, and *excellence* were one of the words in it with its history, meaning, and lack of meaning clearly set down— I am convinced that this alone would knock the legs from under the destructive force in the word.

The several suggestions I've just made all depend in one way or another on increasing our consciousness of the words we use every day. Increasing consciousness isn't, I realize, a small matter. But I think it is the answer. Violent word-forces grow in dark places, wilt in the light of consciousness.

Whatever. Since the back side of excellence popped to the front side for me—letting me see, really see, the violence in it—I've known that we do not see words with our eyes only or hear them with our ears only. We see them with our total nervous systems, with the whole of our beings. Because a word is a microcosm of human consciousness, dead words, all words without meaning, reflect and impinge upon our consciousness. Meaningless words float down and into us—as the quiet, unseen fallout of the deadly radioactive isotope, strontium 90, faintly falls into the river that feeds the plankton that feeds the fish that poisons the people who eat them. So, if our words are meaningless, our education will be meaningless, our economic policies will be meaningless, our love, life, and death will be meaningless—all dead things.

Our words, then, are something like atoms in more than one way: we not only use them as symbols for our concepts—we give them the power to explode us into one large, empty mushroom, into a total system of collective meaninglessness. And if such is the case, it is important that we find better ways than we now have for increasing our consciousness of the empty yet powerful words we inhale and exhale every day.

References

Chapter One

Bruner, J. S. *Toward a theory of instruction*. Cambridge, Mass.: Harvard University Press, 1966.

Cross, K. P. *Beyond the open door: New students to higher education*. San Francisco: Jossey-Bass, 1971.

de Beauvoir, S. *The second sex*. New York: Random House, 1974.

Deutsch, M. Role of social classes in language development. *American Journal of Orthopsychiatry*, 1965, *35*(1), 78-88.

Gardner, J. W. *Excellence: Can we be equal and excellent too*. New York: Harper & Row, 1961.

Grubb, W. N., & Lazerson, M. Rally 'round the workplace: Continuities and fallacies in career education. *Harvard Educational Review*, 1975, *45*(4), 451-474.

Hoggart, R. *The uses of literacy: Changing patterns in English mass culture*. Fair Lawn, N. J.: Essential Books, 1957.

Holt, J. *How children fail*. New York: Dell, 1970.

Karabel, J. Community colleges and social stratification. *Harvard Educational Review*, 1972, *42*(4): 521-562.

Schoolboys of Barbiana. [*Letter to a teacher*] (N. Rossi & T. Cole, trans.). New York: Random House, 1970.

Sennett, R., & Cobb, J. *The hidden injuries of class*. New York: Vintage Books, 1973.

Shaughnessy, M. P. Basic writing. In G. Tate (Ed.), *Teaching composition*: *Ten bibliographical essays*. Fort Worth: Texas Christian University Press, 1976.

Trotsky, L. *Literature and revolution* (Ann Arbor paperbacks for the study of communism and Marxism). Ann Arbor: University of Michigan Press, 1960.

Chapter Two

Applebee, A. N. *Tradition and reform in the teaching of English: A history*. Urbana, Ill.: National Council of Teachers of English, 1974.

Berthoff, A. E. The problem of problem solving. *College Composition and Communication*, 1971, *22*(3), 237-242. Also in W. R. Winterowd, *Contemporary rhetoric: A conceptual background with readings*. New York: Harcourt Brace Jovanovich, 1975.

Berthoff, A. E. Response to Janice Lauer, "Counterstatement," May, 1972. *College Composition and Communication,* 1972, *23*(5), 414-416. Also in W. R. Winterowd, *Contemporary rhetoric: A conceptual background with readings.* New York: Harcourt Brace Jovanovich, 1975.

Booth, W. C. *Modern dogma and the rhetoric of assent.* Notre Dame, Ind.: University of Notre Dame Press, 1974.

Chomsky, N. *Language and mind.* New York: Harcourt Brace Jovanovich, 1972.

Corder, J. W. What I learned at school. *College Composition and Communication,* 1975, *26*(4), 330-334.

D'Angelo, F. *A conceptual theory of rhetoric.* Cambridge, Mass.: Winthrop, 1975.

Elbow, P. *Writing without teachers.* New York: Oxford University Press, 1973.

Emig, J. The uses of the unconscious in composing. *College Composition and Communication,* 1964, *15*(1), 6-12.

Frye, N. Literary criticism. In J. E. Thorpe (Ed.), *The aims and methods of scholarship in modern languages and literatures.* New York: Modern Language Association, 1963.

Lauer, J. Heuristics and composition. *College Composition and Communication,* 1970, *21*(5), 396-404. Also in W. R. Winterowd, *Contemporary rhetoric: A conceptual background with readings.* New York: Harcourt Brace Jovanovich, 1975.

Lauer, J. Response to Ann E. Berthoff, "The problem of problem solving." *College Composition and Communication,* 1972, *23*(2), 208-210. Also in W. R. Winterowd, *Contemporary rhetoric: A conceptual background with readings.* New York: Harcourt Brace Jovanovich, 1975.

Moffett, J. *Teaching the universe of discourse.* Boston: Houghton Mifflin, 1968.

Ohmann, R. *English in America: A radical view of the profession.* New York: Oxford University Press, 1976.

Rohman, D. G. Pre-writing: The stage of discovery in the writing process. *College Composition and Communication,* 1965, *16*(2), 106-112.

Rohman, D. G., & Wlecke, A. O. *Pre-writing: The construction and application of models for concept formation in writing.* East Lansing: Michigan State University, U. S. Office of Education Cooperative Research Project No. 2174, 1964. (ERIC: ED 001 273)

Steinley, G. Introductory remarks on narratology. *College English,* 1976, *38*(3), 311-315.

Warnock, J. New rhetoric and the grammar of pedagogy. *Freshman English News,* 1976, *5*, 1-22. (a)

Warnock, J. Who's afraid of theory? *College Composition and Communication,* 1976, *27*(1), 16-20. (b)

Winterowd, W. R. *Rhetoric: A synthesis.* New York: Holt, Rinehart & Winston, 1968.

Winterowd, W. R. (Ed.). *Contemporary rhetoric: A conceptual background with readings.* New York: Harcourt Brace Jovanovich, 1975.

Winterowd, W. R. Linguistics and composition. In G. Tate (Ed.), *Teaching composition: Ten bibliographical essays.* Fort Worth: Texas Christian University Press, 1976.

Young, R. E., Becker, A. L., & Pike, K. L. *Rhetoric: Discovery and change.* New York: Harcourt, Brace & World, 1970.

Chapter Three

Arnheim, R. *Psychology of art.* Los Angeles: University of California Press, 1966.

Booth, W. *The rhetoric of fiction.* Chicago: University of Chicago Press, 1961.

Lesser, S. O. *Fiction and the unconscious.* Boston: Beacon Hill, 1957.

Lucas, F. L. *Literature and psychology.* Ann Arbor, Mich.: Ann Arbor Paper Backs, 1957.

Chapter Four

Clark, P. P. Critical thinking. *College English*, 1976, *38*(3), 224-233.

Coles, W. E., Jr. Freshman composition: The circle of unbelief. In L. F. Dean, W. Gibson, & K. G. Wilson (Eds.), *The play of language* (3rd ed.). New York: Oxford University Press, 1971.

Chapter Five

Cawelti, J. G. *Adventure, mystery, and romance: Formula stories as art and popular culture.* Chicago: University of Chicago Press, 1976.

Cross, K. P. *Beyond the open door: New students to higher education.* San Francisco: Jossey-Bass, 1971.

Gans, H. *Popular culture and high culture.* New York: Doubleday, 1966.

Perrine, L. *Story and structure.* New York: Harcourt, Brace & World, 1959.

Russ, J. The modern Gothic. *Journal of Popular Culture*, 1972, *6*, 666-691.

Chapter Six

Astrov, M. (Ed.). *American Indian prose and poetry: An anthology.* New York: John Day, 1972.

Brown, D. *Bury my heart at Wounded Knee.* New York: Holt, Rinehart & Winston, 1970.

A conversation with N. Scott Momaday. *Sun Tracks*, Spring 1976, pp. 18-21.

Deloria, V., Jr. *Custer died for your sins.* New York: Macmillan, 1969.

Momaday, N. S. *House made of dawn.* New York: Harper & Row, 1968.

Momaday, N. S. *The way to Rainy Mountain.* Albuquerque: University of New Mexico Press, 1969.

Neihardt, J. G. *Black Elk speaks.* Lincoln: University of Nebraska Press, 1961.

Niatum, D. (Ed.). *Carriers of the dream wheel.* New York: Harper & Row, 1975.

Rosen, K. (Ed.). *The man to send rain clouds: Contemporary stories by American Indians.* New York: Viking Press, 1974.

Rosen, K. (Ed.). *Voices of the rainbow.* New York: Viking Press, 1975.

Roszak, T. *Where the wasteland ends: Politics and transcendance in post-industrial society.* Garden City, N. Y.: Anchor, 1973.

Rothenberg, J. *Shaking the pumpkin: Traditional poetry of the Indian North Americas.* Garden City, N. Y.: Doubleday, 1972.

Silko, L. *Laguna woman.* Greenfield, N. Y.: Greenfield Review Press, 1974.

Silko, L. *Ceremony.* New York: Viking Press, 1977.

Welch, J. *Winter in the blood.* New York: Harper & Row, 1974.

Whorf, B. L. The relation of habitual thought and behavior to language. In J. B. Carroll (Ed.), *Language, thought and reality.* New York: John Wiley, 1959.

Chapter Eight

Booth, W. *The rhetoric of fiction.* Chicago: University of Chicago Press, 1961.

Booth, W. *Modern dogma and the rhetoric of assent.* Notre Dame, Ind.: University of Notre Dame Press, 1974.

Clark, B. *Educating the expert society.* Scranton, Pa.: Chandler, n.d.

D'Angelo, F. *A conceptual theory of rhetoric.* Cambridge, Mass.: Winthrop, 1975.

Dixon, J. *Growth through English* (3rd ed.). Urbana, Ill.: National Council of Teachers of English, 1975.

Gibson, W. *Tough, sweet, and stuffy: An essay on modern American prose styles.* Bloomington: Indiana University Press, 1966.

Kohlberg, L. Stages of moral development as a basis for moral education. In C. M. Beck et al. (Eds.), *Moral education: Interdisciplinary approaches.* Toronto: University of Toronto Press, 1971.

Kohlberg, L. Moral states and moralization: The cognitive-developmental approach. In Thomas Lickona (Ed.), *Moral development and behavior: Theory, research, and social issues.* New York: Holt, Rinehart & Winston, 1976.

Ohmann, R. *English in America: A radical view of the profession.* New York: Oxford University Press, 1976.

Chapter Nine

Bridgman, P. W. *The way things are.* Cambridge, Mass.: Harvard University Press, 1959.

Conant, J. B. The changing scientific scene, 1900–1950. In W. Gibson (Ed.), *The limits of language.* New York: Hill & Wang, 1962.

Dean, L. F., Gibson, W., & Wilson, K. G. (Eds.). *The play of language* (3rd ed.). New York: Oxford University Press, 1971.

DeMott, B. *Supergrow: essays and reports on imagination in America.* New York: E. P. Dutton, 1969.

Gibson, W. (Ed.). *The limits of language*. New York: Hill & Wang, 1962.

Gibson, W. Play and the teaching of writing. In L. F. Dean, W. Gibson, & K. G. Wilson (Eds.), *The play of language* (3rd ed.). New York: Oxford University Press, 1971.

Hall, E. T. *The silent language*. Garden City, N. Y.: Doubleday, 1959.

McLuhan, M. *The Gutenberg galaxy: The making of typographic man*. Toronto: University of Toronto Press, 1962.

Chapter Ten

Brown, R. *A first language: The early stages*. Cambridge, Mass.: Harvard University Press, 1973.

Bruner, J. S., Oliver, R. R., & Greenfield, P. M. *Studies in cognitive growth*. New York: John Wiley, 1966.

D'Angelo, F. *A conceptual theory of rhetoric*. Cambridge, Mass.: Winthrop, 1975.

D'Angelo, F. The search for intelligible structure in the teaching of composition. *College Composition and Communication*, 1976, 27(2), 142–147.

Flavell, J. H. *The developmental psychology of Jean Piaget*. Princeton, N. J.: Van Nostrand, 1963.

Inhelder, B., & Piaget, J. [*The early growth of logic in the child: Classification and seriation*] (E. A. Lunzer & D. Papert, trans.). New York: Harper & Row, 1964.

Lenneberg, E. H. *Biological foundations of language*. New York: John Wiley, 1967.

Nelson, K. Some evidence for the cognitive primacy of categorization and its functional basis. *Merrill-Palmer Quarterly of Behavior and Development*, 1973, *19*, 28.

Piaget, J. [*The origins of intelligence in children*] (M. Cook, trans.). New York: International University, 1952.

Piaget, J. [*The principles of genetic epistemology*] (W. Mays, trans.). London: Routledge & Kegan Paul, 1972.

Ricciuti, H. N. Object grouping and selective ordering behavior in infants 12 to 24 months old. *Merrill-Palmer Quarterly of Behavior and Development*, 1965, *11*, 129, 144.

Slobin, D. I. Developmental psycholinguistics. In W. O. Dinwall (Ed.), *A survey of linguistic science*. Stamford, Conn.: Greylock, 1976.

Chapter Eleven

Arber, A. *The natural philosophy of plant form*. New York: Cambridge University Press, 1950.

Arber, A. *The mind and the eye*. New York: Cambridge University Press, 1954.

Barfield, O. *Saving the appearances: A study in idolatry*. New York: Harcourt Brace Jovanovich, 1965.

Barfield, O. *Poetic diction: A study in meaning* (3rd ed.). Middletown, Conn.: Wesleyan University Press, 1973.

Burnshaw, S. *The seamless web.* New York: Braziller, 1970.

Coleridge, S. T. *Biographia literaria* (J. Shawcross, Ed.). New York: Oxford University Press, 1907.

Coleridge, S. T. *The friend* (Bollingen series; B. Rooke et al., Eds.). Princeton, N.J.: Princeton University Press, 1969.

D'Angelo, F. *A conceptual theory of rhetoric.* Cambridge, Mass.: Winthrop, 1975.

Needham, J. *Moulds of understanding: A pattern of natural philosophy.* New York: St. Martin, 1976.

Needham, J. *Science and civilization in China* (Vol. 5). New York: Cambridge University Press, 1976.

Ohmann, R. *English in America: A radical view of the profession.* New York: Oxford University Press, 1976.

Polanyi, M. *The tacit dimension.* Garden City, N.Y.: Doubleday, 1967.

Polanyi, M. *Personal knowledge: Towards a post-critical philosophy.* Chicago: University of Chicago Press, 1974.

Sewell, E. *The structure of poetry.* Folcroft, Pa.: Folcroft, 1951.

Sewell, E. *The field of nonsense.* Folcroft, Pa.: Folcroft, 1952.

Sewell, E. *The Orphic voice: Poetry and natural history.* New York: Harper & Row, 1971.

Thompson, D. *On growth and form.* New York: Cambridge University Press, 1952.

Whyte, L. L. *Aspects of form.* Bloomington: Indiana University Press, 1961.

Whyte, L. L. *Internal factors in evolution.* New York: Braziller, 1965.

Whyte, L. L. *The universe of experience: A world view beyond science and religion.* New York: Harper & Row, 1974.

Woodger, J. H. *Biology and language.* New York: Cambridge University Press, 1952.

Contributors

Susan R. Blau is Associate Professor at Middlesex Community College in Bedford, Massachusetts, and has been teaching American literature and an introductory course in poetry for eight years. Prior to entering the community college classroom, she taught high school English.

James R. Doherty is Assistant Professor of English, Onondaga Community College, Syracuse, New York. He previously taught English at Grahm Junior College and Bristol Community College, both in Massachusetts.

Theresa L. Enroth has been a faculty member at American River College in Sacramento, California, for eleven years. During this time she has done independent study at the University of Nottingham, England, participated in the Sources of Poetry summer program at Radcliffe College, and taught English as a Second Language on a one-year leave of absence in São Paulo, Brazil. She is presently writing a textbook for an introductory course in poetry.

Walker Gibson has been Professor of English at the University of Massachusetts since 1967 and has been teaching college English since 1946. In 1976-77 he was director of the Fellowships in Residence Program for College Teachers, National Endowment for the Humanities—the program that was the source of this collection of essays. Gibson has written *Tough, Sweet, and Stuffy: An Essay on Modern American Prose Styles* and nine other books, including collections of original poetry.

Thomas C. Gorzycki is Instructor of English at San Jacinto College, Pasadena, Texas. He was formerly a high school English department head in Houston and an instructor of English at Labette Community College in Parsons, Kansas, at which time he received a National Defense of Educational Assistance grant to study generative linguistics and rhetoric at the University of Texas.

Ed Hancock has taught at the University of Dubuque and the University of Nevada and is now in his fourth year of teaching freshman composition and remedial English at Western Nevada Community College, Carson City. He has published *Techniques for Understanding Literature* and is coauthor, with Sheila Hancock, of *Connections: Ideas for Writing.*

David E. Jones is Assistant Professor of English at Los Angeles Valley College, Van Nuys, California. He has also taught at California State College at Los

Angeles, Kent State University, and the University of Akron. His publications include journal articles on "The Essence of Beauty in James Joyce's Aesthetics" and "Spatial Relations in Joyce's *Portrait.*"

James J. Kinney is Assistant Professor of English at Virginia Commonwealth University. He teaches rhetoric, composition, and American literature and supervises graduate students in teaching internships. He also serves as coordinator of the Community College Option, graduate programs in English and Education, and serves as liaison with all community colleges in the state. He has taught at the University of Florida and at Columbia State Community College in Tennessee, where he conducted classes in mass media and the popular arts and served as chair of the Division of Humanities.

Craig Lesley has been an Instructor of English at Clackamas Community College in Oregon City, Oregon, for five years. Recently he spent a one-year sabbatical in the Master of Fine Arts—Fiction program at the University of Massachusetts. He is writing a collection of short stories and is compiling an anthology of contemporary Native American writers for classroom use and the general public. His short story "Spurs" was published in *Writers Forum.* The story's protagonist—an Indian rodeo rider—is modeled after Henry Realbird, who is quoted in Lesley's essay in this book.

Marsha M. Oliver has been a faculty member for ten years at Anoka-Ramsey Community College, Coon Rapids, Minnesota. She teaches college composition, remedial composition, remedial reading, and courses in popular literature. Before engaging in college teaching and remedial work, she was a teacher of high school English. She is working on a textbook about mystery fiction, designed for inexperienced readers.

Arnold T. Orza is Associate Professor of English at the University of Connecticut at Hartford and chairman of the Mansfield Board of Education. He also serves as a consultant to the Fellowship and Media Grants Divisions of the National Endowment for the Humanities and to the Connecticut Council on the Humanities. His publications include several reviews of books on Romantic and Victorian poets.

Peter J. Petersen teaches English at Shasta College, Redding, California.

John Scally is Associate Professor in the Department of Languages and Literature, Ferris State College, Big Rapids, Michigan. He is a recipient of a grant from the National Endowment for the Humanities for "Coordinated Studies in a Technical Curriculum." He has conducted summer seminars for Central Michigan University on "Alternatives in Teaching Composition" and has served as consultant for the Michigan Department of Education. He is familiar with the electronic media, having been executive producer of a nationally broadcast television documentary and a writer and research consultant for a videotape documentary on aging.